P9-COP-066

YOU CAN'T FIRE EVERYONE

YOU CAN'T FIRE EVERYONE

And Other Lessons from an Accidental Manager

HANK GILMAN

PORTFOLIO / PENGUIN

PORTFOLIO / PENGUIN
Published by the Penguin Group
Penguin Group (USA) Inc., 375 Hudson Street,
New York, New York 10014, U.S.A.
Penguin Group (Canada), 90 Eglinton Avenue East, Suite 700,
Toronto, Ontario, Canada M4P 2Y3
(a division of Pearson Penguin Canada Inc.)
Penguin Books Ltd, 80 Strand, London WC2R 0RL, England
Penguin Ireland, 25 St. Stephen's Green, Dublin 2, Ireland
(a division of Penguin Books Ltd)
Penguin Books Australia Ltd, 250 Camberwell Road, Camberwell,
Victoria 3124, Australia
(a division of Pearson Australia Group Pty Ltd)
Penguin Books India Pvt Ltd, 11 Community Centre, Panchsheel Park,
New Delhi – 110 017, India
Penguin Group (NZ), 67 Apollo Drive, Rosedale, North Shore 0632,
New Zealand (a division of Pearson New Zealand Ltd)
Penguin Books (South Africa) (Pty) Ltd, 24 Sturdee Avenue,
Rosebank, Johannesburg 2196, South Africa

Penguin Books Ltd, Registered Offices:
80 Strand, London WC2R 0RL, England

First published in 2011 by Portfolio / Penguin,
a member of Penguin Group (USA) Inc.

1 3 5 7 9 10 8 6 4 2

LIBRARY OF CONGRESS CATALOGING IN PUBLICATION DATA
Gilman, Hank.
You can't fire everyone : and other lessons from an accidental manager / Hank Gilman.
p. cm.
Includes index.
ISBN 978-1-59184-378-8
1. Supervision of employees. 2. Management. 3. Interpersonal relations. I. Title.
HF5549.12.G556 2011
658.3—dc22
2010039734

Printed in the United States of America
Set in Sentinel Book • Designed by Sabrina Bowers

For Catherine, Kevin, Eddie, and Kyle
(in order of appearance)

CONTENTS

Author's Note

I'm always impressed with authors who can totally reproduce conversations, word for word, from two decades ago. I've tried to figure out how they do it. The only way I can think of is that they went through life expecting to write a book. So they either took good notes or carried a tape recorder with them—and had it on most of the time. They also spent a lot of money on batteries. I guess this is possible, but I never did it.

The conversations in this book are reproduced based on fragments of conversations. In other words: they're probably not 100 percent accurate, but they do indeed capture the essence of the exchange between the subject and me.

Also: some of the names of the people who appear in this book have been changed. I use real names when the person is a quasi-public figure, or when I say something—or describe a scene—that makes them look good. As I say in the introduction, I'm not keen on making anyone look bad or giving them the TMZ treatment unless it's necessary. I'm not writing about politicians or celebrities, after all. Not that they deserve to be ridiculed either. I certainly don't mind making myself look bad. And that does happen. You'll see if you get that far.

Introduction

☛ If you like this book, thank the Internet. If you hate it, blame the Internet. A few years ago, I was pondering my future and thinking about the pathetic state of print journalism and the slow death of anything resembling serious reporting in the age of the blog. Was my career, at fifty-six, at an end? Was I a dinosaur unwilling to come to grips with the new world order in my business? Great jobs at *The Wall Street Journal, The Boston Globe, Newsweek,* and *Fortune* aside, was it all a waste? I wondered if I could survive in a world of recycled stories and waterskiing squirrels. (If you don't know what I'm talking about, Google "Twiggy the Waterskiing Squirrel" and you'll understand exactly why I was so afraid.) Had I done anything worthwhile all these years outside of making a damn good living? What was my exit plan?

If you know anything about journalists, you know they always think about exit plans. Even before the Internet, Facebook, and Twitter, we were paranoid about losing our jobs. We always have been insecure. Many of us turn to jobs in the public relations business because we think that the skills are somehow the same—writing and talking. But it rarely works well. Ex-reporters, because they're embarrassed that they left the profession, tend to spend the first part of their pitch explaining to you that they used to be journalists, as if you're going to run a lousy story because you feel some bond with them. Real PR people do not apologize for what they do.

But PR was never for me. It's too corporate, and I'm not polished enough to have to present myself to people all day. I don't dress well, most of the time I don't use the right fork, and I rarely talk in complete sentences.

Writing a book is another popular exit strategy for journalists. I've always avoided writing a book because there are so many bad ones out there. I came close once, hoping to write a biography of Sam Walton, the founder of Wal-Mart, before someone, one of my bosses, in fact, beat me to it.

So why did I write this book? Is this my exit strategy? Well, no. I decided to write a book because I found a topic that I both understood and cared about: management. I basically did an inventory of my career. I've been a rock-solid, major-league journalist at some of the best publications known to man. I didn't win the Pulitzer Prize, but, then again, Ted Williams never won a World Series. The people I worked with—and helped—brought home some pretty nice trophies, though. So maybe I had something to do with that? I was a good coach; a good editor, working with living legends like Jane Bryant Quinn and Robert Samuelson of *Newsweek* and Allan Sloan, now at *Fortune*. Maybe there was a book to do about being a good boss? My business was perfect fodder. It was, and is, in turmoil and filled with volatile and creative—and sometimes really mean—people. The ultimate management lab. The challenges have never been greater in this or any other industry under siege: publications are slashing budgets and staff in an effort to stay afloat and employees on my watch are scared and skeptical because the traditional media business is falling apart. If they lost their jobs, how else were they going to make a living? Working at Ace Hardware? (Though I do like Ace Hardware.)

So after mulling this over a bit, I jotted down what I know about managing people. It isn't as easy as you think. If any human resources type could be honest with you for a second, they'd tell you their company was filled with folks who have no clue how to be good bosses and make their people better at what they do. They scream, discourage, hire the wrong people, take all the credit for great work, and blame their employees for their own mistakes. Most of them don't even know how to fire someone the right way. Some of this misbehavior can be blamed on really warped personalities. But the biggest problem is that no one ever trained them how to be good bosses—or any sort of bosses, for that matter.

How bad is it? In my business, which you will hear a whole lot about in this book, we find bosses by taking talented writers, waving a wand and saying, "Hey, congratulations, you're now supervising a dozen people. And by the way, good luck." Let me tell you, good editors and good writers are not the same thing. You get lucky a lot—after all, these are smart folks who can figure anything out eventually. But this strategy often ends up in disaster. Think about it: a reporter is basically a loner who cares about his own work and no one else's. Is that what you want from a boss? I'm sure it's the same in other industries. The super salesperson doesn't necessarily make a great sales manager. The Boston Celtics basketball great Bill Russell—more on him later—wasn't a particularly a good coach, unless he was playing for himself. He couldn't, it seemed, understand why his players didn't think about the game—and execute—the way he did. Superstars in any line of work are often that way.

So with all that in mind, I'm going to give you advice in this book about being a boss and tell a lot of war stories along the way. This will be a jargon-free zone. In other words: if you like reading about things such as "thought leadership," put this book back on the shelf immediately. I will make fun of people from time to time and quote some folks you might not expect to hear from on the subject of management. I am not, however, going to say nasty things about people I've worked with. Well, for the most part. Not only do I have little desire to ask them for comment, but, well, we all have flaws.

Which brings me to one of the central points of this book. If you get nothing else from my rants, just hold on to the idea that everyone who works for you has flaws. To be a good manager, you've got to work with these imperfect people and figure out a way to avoid their weaknesses. You have to take what they do well and let them do it. Forget about asking some guy who can't dunk to dunk a basketball. For some reason, we're always asking the short guy to dunk. But maybe he's a good three-point shooter. Let him do that! And you know what else? You can't get rid of everybody, so you better figure out what your troops do well. (Former General Electric chief Jack Welch was, among other things, known for a scheme in which he would lop off the lower portion of his workforce—the "C's"—every year. Good luck with that. What if the "C" has a crucial single skill? What if you have a workforce so obsessed with this process that they get distracted from their actual jobs? Just asking.)

I know it's lame to use sports analogies, but managing is really like being a coach: you have to put together a team of wildly disparate parts and get them all to work toward a single goal. (Management jargon. Sorry!)

But before we get started, a little about me. From high school on, I always wanted to be in the journalism business. My parents, believe it or not, had at least five newspapers delivered to our home every day. I loved information and I loved finding out about things. I wanted to know the story behind the story. How things really worked. And I didn't want to be trapped in any single profession. In college, all my friends in business school knew everything any human would want to know about marketing, but nothing else. I wanted to know about marketing and *everything* else. I wasn't disappointed. My first job as a reporter was at *The Beaufort* (South Carolina) *Gazette*. I learned everything from Marine Corps basic training rules to what sewer commissions discuss at their meetings (nothing interesting) to what makes a good Miss Universe contestant (guess) to how to grow Beaufort County's largest watermelon (patience and good fertilizer).

I learned a lot of things along the way, including how to be a better reporter. But I have to make a confession. Nobody trained me to be a boss. I learned on the job and made a lot of mistakes. I still make a lot of mistakes. For some reason, though, I knew I had the boss gene and stuck with it. One day, back in the eighties, I was walking across the Brooklyn Bridge with my friend Walt Bogdanich. For those of you who don't know him, he's one of the greatest journalists of my generation. He's won a slew of Pulitzer Prizes, among many other awards in both print and broadcast. And he'll win a few more, I'm sure. (Somebody should write a book about him.)

We were talking, as we walked the bridge, about a story he

was reporting on blood testing labs, which would eventually earn Walt his first Pulitzer. We worked at *The Wall Street Journal* at the time and we strategized how to shape the series so he could get the maximum clout for what was a pretty important story. Trust me, journalists in real life don't get pumped up about their colleagues' stories. We're petty and jealous. But I really enjoyed my conversations with Walt and found I could be somewhat helpful. Other times I just listened, offered a suggestion or two, and that was enough. I kind of liked that, and even though he and I were just friends, that's what managing is about. It can be that simple.

Of course, there are a lot of other things that go into being a good editor/manager. You have to have the ability to fix bad work without destroying the writer's confidence. You have to spot potential legal problems. You have to keep your writers focused on the conceit of the story and help them develop a strategy for reporting it. You have to help them with their careers, identifying the next step and helping them achieve that goal. It took me years to learn all that. It took me literally minutes to learn not all reporters were like Walt.

My first shot at running people was at *The Boston Globe,* around 1988. An assistant editor's job was opening up in the business section, and even though I thought I might be throwing away a writing career, I was interested. Another friend, a great boss herself now, told me that if it didn't work out, it would be, at least, "another arrow in my quiver." That made sense to me. I took her advice, took the job and dived in. Boy, was I unprepared. All of a sudden, I was responsible for about two dozen people—not just myself. Former friends became enemies (don't miss that chapter!). I had no idea how to hire good people. And I had no idea how to fire the bad ones that no one had the guts to fire before I took the job. But hell, it was fun making decisions, having people pretend they liked you and your bad jokes—and being an editor paid a lot better.

So, for two decades now—starting with the *Globe*, then *Newsweek*, and then the great *Fortune* magazine (my current employer, at least as I write this)—I have played the part of boss and have actually become, I think, one of the better managers/editors/bosses/psychologists in my business. I've worked with, and for, some of the biggest names in journalism. The writers in my world have won lifetime achievement awards and many of the highest honors in the business. As a writer, I have observed and written about some of the best managers and business folks ever—from Sam Walton, the founder of Wal-Mart, and Charles Lazarus, the founder of Toys "R" Us, to the young Bill Gates who would, in the late eighties, come into our offices at *The Wall Street Journal* to chat about Microsoft, grab a cup of coffee, and make fun of IBM and other tech types..

But enough about me. This is a book for you. I hope you enjoy it and, as a result, make fewer mistakes than I did.

HANK GILMAN

Friendless

•

LONELINESS IS THE PENALTY OF LEADERSHIP.

SIR ERNEST SHACKLETON, ANTARCTIC EXPLORER

☛ Sir Ernest sure wasn't kidding.

Sometimes I wish I worked at Dunder Mifflin—you know, the fictional paper company portrayed on the TV show *The Office*. Michael Scott, the boss in the Scranton, Pennsylvania, branch where much of the show takes place, gets drunk with his employees, goes out to Japanese steak houses and picks up waitresses with them, and even tells foul jokes at work with just a slap on the wrist from corporate HR. "My number one job," Michael, portrayed by Steve Carell, tells a new employee in one episode, "is being your friend." If only. Every time I watch Michael in action I cringe, because I know everything he does always seems to end up in disaster. Plus, it reminds me that I can never, ever, have those types of relationships with my employees—or even try. Nor can you, for the most part, because, no matter what you do, it's frequently going to end up a mess.

Just the other day I was having lunch with one of my editors at *Fortune*. I was telling him how I felt I was going to end my career old and friendless because I've fired way too many people. "Everybody hates me," I said. He said it was true; "a lot of people hate you."

You should never try to be Michael. For the most part, you

can never have good, close friends on your staff once you start being their boss. If you're doing your job the way you're supposed to, you'll invariably do something to fracture the relationship. You'll give someone a bad review; you'll pass them up for a promotion; you won't smile enough when you open their holiday gift; you'll fire them. Something will come up. If you don't do any of these things because you're afraid of the fallout, then you're *really* not doing your job and the Scranton office will get shut down.

To prove that I know what I'm talking about, let me tell you a few stories. In each case, I learned something about being a boss and supervising old and new pals. I'm writing this from the perspective of a guy who was promoted--without much thought; I can guarantee that--into a supervisory job. It's happened a few times in my career. In college, at journalism school. Once when I was promoted into management from the reporters' ranks at *The Boston Globe*. And once when I rejoined *Fortune* in a position above former peers. In both cases, it was awkward at the beginning. In both cases I realized early on that my job, not the friendships, came first.

But, rest assured, there's kind of a happy ending to both of these stories. I discovered I didn't have to be totally friendless—though I do have a lot fewer buddies than I did when I was a young soldier in the trenches bitching about management. But what the hell. I own a bigger house now and my family still likes me. I guess.

The Newbie

This story begins at the University of South Carolina College of Journalism. This was back in the seventies, kids, when newspapers ruled and you actually had to get cash from bank and supermarket tellers. I was a student in a senior semester class where, as part of our assignment, we produced a weekly newspaper. I, for some reason, was chosen as the chief of one of the editions. One professor, Henry Price, later said he and the other teachers "saw something" in me. I never got a fuller explanation, but this was a time in history when people actually thought they liked folk music, if you know what I mean. So there was no telling what condition they were in. In any event, it was a mini-disaster. I essentially let my friends do whatever they wanted to do. And they did: they rarely showed up to class, and when they did, they basically refused to work. They had a great time because I did all the work in a desperate effort to pick up their slack. I learned a big lesson back in 1975: it's either you or them—and I'd rather it be them. In other words: If I let my friends get away with not working, it would be me who would get the "F." I don't think I remained friends with a single one of them.

When I finally graduated, I worked for a series of newspapers as a reporter. I never gave much thought to editing and largely ignored editors except when they tortured me. In the late seventies, I worked for a small suburban Hartford, Connecticut, newspaper called the *Journal-Inquirer*. While there, the one thing I learned about editing was that it didn't look like a very appealing profession. Editors were stuck in the office all the time and didn't age well. My bosses were either trying to hit on young reporters or complaining that their lives had come to this—a sleepy job in a Manchester, Connecticut, office park fixing bad copy about planning commissions and holiday parades. Few of them had friends in the newsroom. They stood alone at work parties and drank lots of crappy beer. They weren't exactly well liked. At one point, a photo editor sent out a memo to his staff that read: "Effective immediately, the photo staff will no longer refer to the photo editor as 'dickhead.'" True story.

Several years later, I ended up at *The Boston Globe* (after a stint at *The Wall Street Journal*), where I was the personal finance columnist. As I alluded to in the introduction, I eventually took a job as an assistant business editor in charge of the Sunday business section. All my friends in the department were happy. For me, I thought at the time. But maybe they simply thought my appointment meant they could get away with having to do less work. (Hell, I'd think the same thing.) I was a bit wary because I knew what was coming based on my University of South Carolina debacle. Little did my work friends know that I actually intended to do my job. I was tested immediately. A woman I was pretty friendly with covered the tech industry and considered herself an industry guru of sorts. (Most tech writers want to be gurus, not journalists, for some strange reason. Maybe they all fantasize about inventing something like Facebook. Maybe they find the young CEOs more fascinating than their own bosses. That's it! Anyway, a story for another time.) She seemed talented, judging by the articles she wrote. But I soon discovered that you really don't know much about a writer until you see her raw copy—nor do you know much about writers, or anyone else for that matter, until you try to manage them.

The reporter, who I'll call "Jane" (I actually think that's her real name. Oops!), talked a good game and had a lot of swagger. She considered herself a hotshot without actually having the chops to back it up. No problem, right? She turned in a long story about something like the fate of Digital Equipment Corporation, then the world's second largest computer maker, right behind IBM. (And now its remains, I guess, are kept in a cremation urn at Hewlett-Packard.) I had to rewrite the piece and ask a couple of dozen questions because the reporting was filled with sinkholes. I literally thought, "Oh shit. She's my friend. We have lunch together. How is she going to react when I tell her this article is rubbish? Who am I going to have lunch with? Will she uninvite me to her wedding?"

So I made a little calculation, taking a lesson from my days as a "boss" at the University of South Carolina. If I let this go—if I passed this rubbish on to the copydesk and let them deal with it—I would still have a friend and the wedding invitation. But I would eventually be fired—you don't let bad stories get by at what was, at the time, one of the nation's great newspapers. Not to make a friend happy, anyway. Unlike college, there was a salary at stake and my professional reputation, which would take me years to clean up. More important, I was being paid by the *Globe* and was loyal to the guy who gave me the job. The friendship had to go. After the story was published, Jane sent a memo to my boss, Steve Bailey, to complain about the editing process—to complain about me, in other words. She said that my questions were "gratuitous." (I think she said "idiotic," too, but I can't be sure. Probably.) Steve knew better. I was doing my job and, as a result, passed my first test. He trusted me from that point on and the rest of the staff got the message that, as long as I was in charge, the newspaper would come first and they would come second—no matter how much I personally liked all of them. And, by the way, I still got to go to the wedding. Although I think I was sitting in the back at a card table with a white tablecloth thrown over it.

Hiring Friends? Mostly, Not a Good Idea

As soon as you become a boss, you have the power to make some people happy, especially your friends and friends of your friends. In good times, you have jobs and freelance work to dole out and, trust me, old pals will ask you for work. But you'll soon learn there are two ways to lose friends in this process: 1. You give work to people who aren't that talented—and then you have to fire them; 2. You know they're bad and refuse to give them work—and they end up firing you, in a way, by ending the friendship. Either way, your roster of relationships gets smaller.

I want to introduce you to an ex-pal called "Ugly Al." I call him that because he was truly unpleasant to look at. He had a receding hairline with a large forehead and eyes that just bugged out at you. He should have worn a goalie mask like the guy in the *Friday the 13th* movie. I should have known it wouldn't end well. Al fancied himself a writer. In fact, his wife worked hard so he could indulge his fantasy. (I really hate those "writers with hardworking wives" kind of writers.) But, as a friend, I agreed to arrange for some work for him at the *Globe*. As it turned out, not only was he a bad writer but he harassed his editors with frequent phone calls and various demands about his expenses. Every day, it seemed, some editor he was working with would call me and ask what the hell was I thinking by giving this guy work. It was a good question without a good answer.

I called Al and told him that if he agreed never to call the *Globe* again, I would get him his paycheck for no work in return. That solved that problem. The trouble was, I lost the trust of a number of editors at the *Globe*. Why was this a problem? Well, for one thing, you don't want your coworkers badmouthing you. It's not a terrific career move. For another, you may end up working for one of those editors one day. "Hey, good to see you. Aren't you the jerk who hired that ugly guy a few years ago?" ("Yup, that was me. How many weeks of severance do I get?")

Hiring Really Good Friends? *Really* Proceed with Caution

A number of years after I hired and fired Ugly Al, I found myself at a great little magazine called *Fortune Small Business*. I loved running this magazine because I was allowed to do my best work with minimum scrutiny and office politics. It had the feel of a college newspaper. And we were pretty much left to our own devices in the shadow of the mother ship, *Fortune* magazine. We took chances. We succeeded and failed and no one seemed to care. It was paradise for a magazine maker. But it wasn't the easiest place to hire first-rate talent. *FSB*, as we called it, had a circulation of 1 million readers, but it was what is known as a "controlled circulation" publication. That means it was sent free to people—many of whom, one of my bosses pointed out, "drove around with plastic bugs on the top of their cars." My friends called it junk mail—thanks, guys. Some might call it journalism's equivalent of local-access cable. But it was a terrific magazine with a terrific group of engaged readers.

The staff, initially, wasn't all that great. So over time I had to ask a few writers and editors to leave. And some left on their own after they figured out they just didn't fit in. When I was done firing people or scaring them off, which I had to do if there was any hope of improving the magazine, I started hiring. I had a friend at a national publication who had enjoyed working with me in the past and was looking for a change. It appeared on the surface to be a good match. He was a great rewrite editor and idea generator. I figured I had a shot because the work hours were predictable and, because of a family situation, he needed predictable. Now, I knew he was a little prickly—and that he had this Mr. Hyde side, but I thought I could manage that. I was desperate, basically, for a major-league editor. I was, like Sir Ernest Shackleton—alone.

I ended up making a couple of mistakes: First, I ignored the problems he had at his previous employer—stuff like rudeness, sense of entitlement, terrible bedside manner—which came up whenever he was put in a position of modest power. Second, even though we had a flexible schedule, I offered to let him work from home too frequently. Third, I didn't pay enough attention to how he was interacting with the staff. Things seemed to be going well for a few months, but I soon learned that if your employees know the villain is a trusted friend of the boss, they'll never come forward and tell the truth. (The guy's head could be spinning around *Exorcist*-style and they wouldn't say a thing.) Thankfully, in this case, one young reporter couldn't take it anymore.

The reporter was essentially this editor's assistant. One day she came to see me and was clearly upset. The star editor I hired was making her perform a variety of personal chores—visiting the dry cleaner was apparently an important work-related task, as was paying his utility bills. He was also rude, which isn't unusual in this business. But he was rude too often. The abuse was relentless. I told her not to worry. I'd take care of it. I talked with the whole staff and the stories were similar. It was like "Ugly Al" screaming at *The Boston Globe* editors. If I didn't do something about this man, I would run the risk of losing the staff completely, especially my best talent.

I wasn't looking forward to the confrontation. My friend was a great journalist and I'd miss that part. He also had a family and didn't have a whole lot of money. Guilt ahoy. Lucky for me—not for him—the problem was solved by outside forces. *Fortune* was in the middle of layoffs and they wanted me to bring on a couple of talented editors they couldn't carry anymore. I was happy to oblige, but still had to call in my friend and fire him. At first, I was going to chicken out and blame *Fortune*. Yeah, I could have said I was being forced to make room for the new guys. But, in reality, if he had been doing his job well, I would have refused to bring on the *Fortune* refugees and kept him on. So I didn't lie. I ended up telling him the truth because he had to avoid the same mistakes in his next job.

"Why didn't they lay off one of the *Fortune* editors? Why me?" he asked.

"Because," I said, "I would have had to have this conversation with you anyway. You pretty much lost the staff. Not because you're not talented, but because of the way you dealt with *them.*"

I pretty much knew right then that our friendship was over for good. (I think a big clue was the "I'm going to kill you as soon as you turn your back" look he gave me.) We have talked once or twice in the decade since then. But that may be a high estimate. Oh well.

Happy Ending? Uh, It Depends

I've been editing for nearly two decades now and, despite all the various problems I've faced, I have managed to maintain some friendships at work. I go to concerts every once in a while with one of my bosses. I've never asked him, but I think this friendship/work relationship works out okay because we *both* know that someday he'll have to fire me. It's like baseball managers. They all know that they'll eventually be fired, no matter what their relationship with the team's general manager. No hard feelings. Same way with another one of my bosses. Though we've been friends for years—I was actually *his* boss for a while—I know he has to lay down the law, even with me. I have some other friends at work and it does get awkward at times. Recently, another editor complained about one of my friends being a "bitch" to him. I told him that she was a friend but as her supervisor he had to deal with it. Ignore me. Deal with her. (And drop the "bitch" stuff, by the way.)

Most of the time, I just try to keep out of it—unless I have to intervene.

Sometimes I take this hands-off philosophy too far. I once talked a recently hired colleague into giving a friend's daughter an internship. For some reason, he flipped out when she asked for more challenging work. I didn't step in because of the connection. But I should have. Apparently, as I found out later, he also verbally abused his staff on a regular basis. We eventually had to fire him. But if I had been smart, and sensitive to the obvious clues, I should have taken care of the problem right then and there and saved everyone a lot of pain.

When it comes to hiring pals I will only bring in what I call "A" players. That means folks who are at the top of their game. The superstars. I've hired Allan Sloan twice. He's arguably the best business journalist of his generation, or one of a small handful anyway, but he's also a good friend. When I bring someone in for a staff job, I remove myself from the interviewing process. It makes things far less complicated. Of course, it does get a little uncomfortable when you don't come up with work for your "B" friends. A husband of a good friend is constantly pitching me stories. I'm always tempted to run with one of them because I like his wife a lot and want to help her out. But the prospect of killing his story, which I know would happen, keeps me in line. But even those folks suspect you're just doing your job and the really good friends respect that. Many years ago, I tried to get a good pal hired as a writer at Time Inc. He was an "A" player and was close to being hired. He wasn't, for reasons I still can't fathom. But he was a bit sore at me because I knew in advance but didn't give him a heads-up. I was honest about the reason—this was a work situation and I couldn't reveal what my boss was thinking because my boss told me this information in confidence. Our friendship was strained for a while, but he eventually figured out I was just doing my job.

So, can you still remain friends after you fire someone? Yes. It's weird, but possible. I recently had to let a friend go in what has come to seem like our annual purge. I was really dreading it, but he always knew me as a guy who would not play favorites, and I think that made it better. "I really hope," he said, "we get to work with each other again." Go figure. Not that we've seen each other much since then.

A little twist on all this is working with folks who *become* friends when you work with them over the years. It's kind of creepy. You have no idea, after a while, if they go to lunch with you because they like you or because they feel like they have to. (And do they make fun of you when talking with other employees? Sure!) Can you ever trust friends who work for you? I actually think about this and it drives me crazy. When I was sick in the hospital a couple of years ago, I found out who my good friends on the staff were. When I get back from a long vacation and someone seeks me out to talk to me or ask me how I've been, that tells me something, too. But I have a great wife and kids and they keep me busy, so I try not to care too much about what my employees think about me personally. If they think I'm a good boss, that's fine. If not, I can find a couple of new friends someplace else. Dunkin' Donuts counter people are kind of cool.

Even as I've been working on this book, I've found out how many former "friends" actually dislike me. I was attending a party at a rival publishing company, which must hold a record for hiring unemployed journalists. (Bless them.) I saw several people I used to work with. A few of them had, in fact, lost their jobs at *Fortune*. It was a chilly reception for me. One of them was someone I thought was a good friend. I knew his wife well, and we'd socialized from time to time over the years. But apparently he thought I was somehow responsible for his fate at *Fortune*. (I wasn't. And, in fact, I lobbied to save his job on two previous occasions. Ah, the things you don't tell people because they would never want to know.) For the first time in my career as a manager, I was totally snubbed. This guy wouldn't look at me. He wouldn't talk to me even after I walked within a foot of him to say hello. I was kind of hurt, which I suppose will make him happy if he ever reads this book. (Just don't volunteer to review it—okay?) What is the old saying? "If you want a friend, buy a dog"? Yup, that's the lesson, dear readers.

✖

Recruiting and Managing "the Talent"

☛ I'm showing my age here, but the best basketball player I've ever seen in action was Bill Russell, who won eleven championships for the Boston Celtics from the late fifties into the late sixties. He revolutionized the game in many ways, from using shot blocking as an offensive weapon (the fast break) to building the strong concept of the team where everyone sacrifices their own stats and personal glory—though he ended up with a lot of that—for the sake of winning.

Bill was interesting in other ways. (If you want to know more, read a few of his books, which are, in my mind, great histories of both race relations and sports.) He was such an intense player, for example, that he couldn't practice every day like some of his teammates. He needed to rest, mentally and physically. His coach, the legendary Red Auerbach, understood this and let him sit in the stands during practice sipping a cup of tea. No announcements to the press—not that there were many reporters covering the team—that the star player was under the weather and was sent home. No excuses like "Russell sat out of practice today for personal reasons." (In the NFL today, that can mean a "hangover" or "he shot someone in a club and is looking for a place to bury the gun.") No, he just sat in the stands sipping his cup of tea for all to see.

Here's how Russell explained it in his book *Red and Me*: "Eventually tea in the stands became my new routine and I almost never scrimmaged again. Later, I heard from players whose coaches knew about this, and they all thought that Red was kissing my ass. With that narrow frame of reference—which was essentially a pre-conceived notion—they couldn't fathom it because they weren't capable of handling a situation like that with such clarity and wisdom." Russell added: "That was great for me because I hated practice. I thought, 'I already know exactly what I'm doing. Practice is only a drain on my energy.' I found it remarkable that Red not only perceived this about me—without me mentioning it—but found a solution to the problem." And it paid off. Years later, in the 1968–69 season, the Celtics finished fourth in their division and it looked like the dynasty had run its course. But they shocked the NBA—I would say shocked the nation, but no one paid much attention to the NBA in those days—and won the championship under Russell. If it weren't for the "Russell Rules"—these came long before the "Jordan Rules"—it would never have happened. Red was smart enough to make sure his star was rested and ready for the playoffs. And he didn't much care who had a problem with it.

What Red figured out was that dealing with your best employees is the most important part of your job. If you can motivate them, you and your company will do well. And you're going to look great to your bosses. It starts with the recruiting process and never stops. How do you treat them during the courtship? Do you make accommodations? Do you adapt to their work styles? Are you getting the best from them? Red Auerbach was brilliant when dealing with Russell. When he stepped down as coach he offered the job to his best player.

✖

Why? No one else could motivate Russell. He wouldn't play for anyone else. It was the ultimate accommodation. The result: two more years of Russell and two more championships.

There are no set rules for recruiting the best people, coaching stars, and getting the best out of them. But after managing people for several years now, I've figured out a few things—mostly by following my instincts and figuring what worked and what didn't. And trust me, there was a lot of trial and error. I'll talk about finding "the talent" first.

The 24/7 Recruiter

As anyone will tell you, recruiting talent is one of the more important jobs as a manager. The bibles (of management) tell you to spend a certain percentage of your job on recruiting. But that's malarkey. You should be doing this in some way at every moment of every day. (I always love when people tell you that 20 percent of your job should be spent on a certain task. First of all, all the "necessary parts of your job" would add up to 300 percent. I'm not quite sure anyone doling out this advice ever held a real job.) Your pals are always telling you about someone. You're getting a constant stream of résumés—many bad. You're meeting all sorts of people in your business every day. You're reading every day. This is all part of the recruiting process, but being successful at it requires a bit of a more subtle skill. Most of all, you need patience. You also have to be flexible. No grudges if you offer someone a job and they turn you down. They could have a better offer; they could just hate you; it might not be the right time. If you really believe someone will be an asset to your staff, you should let them make their own decisions and be willing to wait for them to come to you.

This concept is evident in my relationship with Allan Sloan, who has worked for me twice now and threatened to work with me on other occasions. I first met Allan in the late eighties. He was working for *Newsday,* a Long Island newspaper, and self-syndicating his column and generally pissing off a whole lot of people like Donald Trump. The best thing about Allan, and there are many, is that he understands numbers as well as the CEOs and their financial teams. He knows what he's talking about, and *they know* he knows what he's talking about. That's a pretty serious skill for a business journalist.

But enough of the digression. When I met Sloan, I was an assistant business editor at *The Boston Globe* and was among his early customers for his syndicated column. I had seen his work in *Newsday,* and I always thought his column was one of the best in journalism, period. But I had no illusions that he would come to work for the *Globe.* (Whenever I meet anyone of extraordinary talent, I try to figure out how to get them to work for me whether I have a chance or not.) But I knew we both had long careers in front of us and told him never to accept another job without talking to me first. And he did just that when a few years later I landed at *Newsweek.* He had decided to leave *Newsday* and I was competing with *Money* magazine for his services. But Allan remembered how comfortable he was working with me at the *Globe* (as a buyer of his column) and I think he appreciated that I was a true fan who valued his work. I also think he thought he made a promise to me.

Strangely, about ten years after I left *Newsweek,* I helped hire Allan again at *Fortune.* My dream was to have Allan and

Carol Loomis, another legendary superstar, in the same workplace at the same time. (That's what amounts to entertainment for me.) I figured if I waited long enough, that would happen. And it did. But in a very strange way. Allan was still at *Newsweek*—he claims I abandoned him—and Andy Serwer, my current boss, was a writer at *Fortune*. They got into a feud, in print and online, over the Time Warner and AOL merger. (Allan said it was a terrible idea and Andy basically said the merger wasn't a great idea, but it wasn't the end of the world.) Then they attacked each other in various ways. Not fun for me, who liked them both a lot.

The details aren't important, but I had a little problem. I knew I wanted Allan to join *Fortune* at some point, and I also knew that it wouldn't happen unless Andy was okay with it. Andy was a big talent at *Fortune* at the time, and any manager with half a brain would want to keep him happy. I had no idea he'd be my boss one day, so I'm glad we did keep him happy. (An important lesson there, kids!) And there was no way in hell Allan would work at *Fortune* if he was still at war with Andy. Now remember, this was years before Allan would ever join *Fortune*. But I had to lay the groundwork. I asked them to join me for lunch at the Gramercy Tavern in New York City. It was pretty tense, but the guys were well behaved and, I think, discovered they had a lot more in common than they thought. They even ordered coffee and dessert. (One thing about business is that you only order coffee and dessert when you're having a pretty good meeting.) I don't think they changed their views on things, but when Andy became *Fortune*'s editor a few years later, I once again organized a meeting between him and Allan. After that first lunch they'd already learned they could work with each other despite their differences. It was, to this day, the best meeting I've ever arranged.

You Can't Always Get What You Want, but Maybe Sometimes

Attracting talent requires compromises.

Consider Jerry Useem, a young star at *Inc.* magazine in Boston in the late nineties. I discovered him when he took on the Harvard Business School in an article about how female MBA students weren't quite comfortable with the school's "frat-house atmosphere." (Judging from the article, the place sounded more like a bad night at the bar at Applebee's.) I read the article on the magazine's Web site and wondered why it didn't appear first in print. As it turned out, the *Globe* was coming out with an article as well, tipped off by Harvard, which I was told would be a little more sympathetic to the Ivy's cause. At least that's what *Inc.*'s editors and Jerry thought. So here was young Jerry Useem taking on two big Boston institutions: Harvard and *The Boston Globe.* I had to hire this guy. This kind of guts was, and is, unusual in my business.

Unfortunately, I didn't have the juice. I was editor of *Fortune Small Business* magazine. A great little publication, as I said earlier. But it wasn't a place where a young, ultra-talented journalist aspired to work. I had breakfast in Boston with Jerry, who proceeded to tell me, in so many words, "If I'm going to leave *Inc.*, I want to work for *Fortune.* Not another small business magazine." Translation: "Thanks for the breakfast, but I'm on the fast track and you're the minor leagues." ("And could you pass the jam? I'm in a rush." Jerry didn't say that, but he would have.)

I could understand his perspective. We *weren't* big league enough, it was true, and any talented kid wants to write for the best. I knew this from personal experience after having been, over the years, recruited by a couple of trade publications, which were run by smart people who could have played ball at any level. But I didn't want to leave the majors. The pay would have been higher, the work easier, the tension level lower, and the hours better. But I'd miss the buzz and the impact. I'd miss working really hard and I'd miss my bosses *expecting* me to work really hard. So I knew Jerry was making the same calculation, and I told him that we would stay in touch and, more important, there were no hard feelings. I also told him that I'd haunt him until he came to Time Inc.

I flew back to New York, still trying to figure out how I might one day be able to woo Jerry. I sent his writing samples to my *Fortune* bosses. They loved his work. So I came up with an arrangement that made everyone happy: Time Inc. would hire Jerry to write for *Fortune*, but he would also write a couple of pieces a year for me at *FSB* and *Money* magazine. I was happy because I could get a few good cover stories a year from him—close to what I would get anyway if he were working only for *FSB*—and Jerry was happy because he got to work for *Fortune*, which was a dream job. And he didn't mind writing for me because he actually liked writing about small business.

Of course, I got screwed in the end. *Fortune*'s editors liked Jerry so much that they eventually reneged on the deal and kept him at the magazine full-time. What the hell. I had seen it coming, and after all I did get him to *Fortune* in the first place. But it was one of the hires I was most proud of. The great Jim Collins, the ultimate management guru and a friend of Jerry's, paid me the highest compliment I think I ever received in the business. "Hiring Jerry," he told me, "is like drafting Tom Brady in the sixth round of the NFL draft." (More from Jim later.)

Playing Fair

A few years ago *Fortune* hired from *The Wall Street Journal* Pulitzer Prize winner James Bandler, who was well known for being part of the team that exposed the stock option backdating scandals a few years ago. I think this is a case where patience paid off. I also think it helped that we weren't willing to sling mud at the other publications vying for James's services. That said something good about us.

Not only were we competing against his current employer—one of the best platforms for any journalist in the country—but we also had to battle several other notable publications, including *The New York Times,* which was putting on a full-court press.

James eventually decided to stay at the *Journal* to give the Murdoch administration—they had just bought the newspaper—a chance. Now, there were a couple of ways you could look at this. Some people would say, "Damn, he decided to stay and that's that. Next!" But strangely enough, his decision pleased us. Andy Serwer, my boss, and I knew that as long as he *didn't* go to the *Times,* we'd have a chance to eventually get him. The fact that he wasn't starting a new job meant that whatever reasons he had started flirting with us in the first place were still there. And if he loved the *Times* so much, he would have jumped at the job. We were still in the game.

I kept in touch—a call here and a call there. I didn't think anything would happen that quickly, but only a few months later, James called me. "Is the same offer still on the table?" I said: "Uh, sure."

I heard the *Journal* folks told James he would be "selling himself short" if he went to *Fortune*. (By the way, as someone who once worked there, I knew that the *Journal* views all of its journalism competitors this way, so I wasn't much offended.) But we weren't going to get involved in that game. I just focused on what we could do for James. Plus, I didn't actually believe that our competitors were lazy, lowlife hacks. James ended up choosing us, and I don't think, as I write this, that he has had a regret since. At least he tells me he hasn't. I like to think that part of his decision was that we were the kind of folks he'd be comfortable working for. And part of that was because we weren't angry, nasty, and negative about our competitors.

Be Nice When They Say Good-bye. Then, Recruit Them Again

I know this will come as a shocker—well, to some of you—but eventually new and/or better jobs will come along for your more talented people. Or eventually they'll just get tired of what they're doing (and of you) and will want to experience something else. Or sometimes a job offer will come along and your star won't know whether they want to leave or not. But if and when a star decides to leave, you just have to understand and hope that someday they'll return. And you know what? It does happen. And a lot of it depends on how you act when they leave.

Now, some bosses will hold grudges. Pretty much like a scorned husband or wife. There's one story of a publisher I'll leave unnamed, that will not hire you back if you leave. It's a breakup pure and simple. (My boss kind of feels that way. Jeez, you should see his face when someone leaves. But he always lets them return!) But I like to look at it a different way. The day your best employee comes in with the news that they're moving on is the day you start recruiting them again. A few things to keep in mind:

1. **DON'T BAD-MOUTH THE NEW EMPLOYER.** (See the recruiting section.) This is pretty classless. I once interviewed the late Sam Walton for a story I was writing and he not once said a negative word about his competitors. Hell, you could tell him that Kmart was the worst retailer you have ever seen and how could they compete with the mighty Wal-Mart? And by the way, they say Wal-Mart is run by a bunch of hicks. He wouldn't budge. In fact, he would even go on and on about all the good things Kmart was doing. (Hey, look at that Pennzoil display—you can't do much better than that!) You knew he was fibbing a little bit. But the point was he was taking the high road. And it made him look good.

The same thing is true in any business. One of my employees, late in the courtship stage with a competitor, recently asked me what I thought of the people he might be working for. I knew their flaws (I actually thought they were evil trolls), but it wasn't worth getting into. For one thing, he might like the trolls. For another, it would make me look like a petty jerk if I started gossiping about people, some of whom I didn't know. (Not that I'm always above that.) Whenever I hear one of my bosses slander someone, I figure they probably do the same to me as well. So here's my standard line: "Look, you're lucky, you have two good options and you can't go wrong. Of course, I want you to stay. But that's your decision. I have a pony in the race." I actually believe that.

2. COME UP WITH A COUNTEROFFER, BUT ONLY IF THEY REALLY WANT ONE. I tell this to people all the time. If it's partly about money, I'll get you some more. If it's about your title, we can do something about that. (It's only words.) But if you really want a new job—or need a change—take it. You'll be coming back to me anyway in six months if your idea of a good career move is a useless new title.

One of our more talented writers must have gone through this process three or four times before he eventually left. You know, walk in to me or one of his other bosses with a job offer in his hand. He'd come in and say he was being courted and we'd come up with more money. Then he'd come in again. The final time I just said, "Look, it sounds like a great job and I know you need a change of scenery. You're bored. This is the only place you've ever worked. Go off, enjoy the new place, but think of us when you want to come back again. You still have a home here." So he took the new job. I later found out he was insulted that there was no counteroffer—also that I wasn't, no kidding, devastated enough at the thought of his leaving—even though he didn't want a counteroffer and was going to leave anyway. Sometimes you can't win. (Postscript: By the time you read this, the writer may have returned. The grass isn't always greener, but sometimes you just have to let them find that out on their own.)

3. DON'T BE A HYPOCRITE. I've had, let's see, about six or seven major jobs depending upon how you count them up. I'm not going to sit there and tell someone that moving on is a bad thing when it isn't, and I've jumped around a lot. I wouldn't be writing this book if I hadn't had all those jobs, met all those people, and managed in more than one place. And my employees know that, too. It makes it easier to lose someone because you understandand it's just something they have to do. This is especially true of young writers and editors who have been at the same place most of their careers. Trust me, they'll want to work for you again if you're honest and helpful. Unless, of course, you're the reason they're leaving.

But having a lot of different jobs, as a manager, does have some advantages. I can, and do, tell employees with wandering eyes that I've been there. "Go off and have a great time. Enjoy the job. I've had enough of them and you're not going to get much better than this." And I believe that. And, again, sometimes they just need a change. A kind of young reporter left *Fortune* recently to go to *The Washington Post.* I knew she wanted the change partly because she wanted to work in a newsroom atmosphere. No way could we provide that for her. Sometimes you just say good luck, "I know you'll do great," and let them explore what's out there.

4. KEEP IN TOUCH. Of course, you always tell them they can come back. But the hardest part is keeping up connections. I always make it a point to have lunch or dinner and remain friendly. Sometimes they don't come back. But keeping in touch works in other ways. You have a scout in a new place if you want to recruit one of their colleagues. You also have a damn good reference in case you decide you need to look for work! (Hey, don't think it doesn't help.) Finally, former employees are, of course, asked by potential new hires what it is like working for you. And they'll be honest.

Keep the Stars Happy

Recruiting, of course, is the fun part. The hardest part of the job is making sure your most important employees—especially the stars—stay happy and you get the most out of them. It's the Red Auerbach/Bill Russell/cup-of-tea-at-practice rule: stars are different, treat them that way. Now, some people will tell you that you should treat everyone the same. Of course, you shouldn't! That's a bunch of ridiculous blather. If you followed this rule to the teeth, you would pay everyone the same and it would be one happy socialist workplace and, as Garrison Keillor might say, a cheerful place "where all the children are above average." The least talented would get the same assignments as the most talented workers, for example, and you would spend most of your time fixing bad or mediocre work. Your customers would head elsewhere. So stop pretending. First of all, it's okay to treat the stars differently. Some might not understand, but the kids with raw talent will see this and aspire to it. The rest can just leave or complain. That's okay, too. (When I was a young reporter I noticed stars were treated a bit differently. Made sense to me—why the hell would

I want to move up the food chain if there weren't perks? And besides, they did most of the work.)

Now, I'm not talking about free vacations, spin classes, and behind-the-back cash payments. (Though now that I think about that last one . . .) You can usually keep your stars happy with less controversial accommodations such as working at home, a little extra time off here and there, and a nicer office. More important than anything is making sure their work is interesting. As long as the results are good, I don't care. Your stars do the best work, typically are the hardest workers, and tackle the projects with the highest degree of difficulty. They're also a rare commodity. There are plenty of people out there with some level of talent—and you can hire as many as you want, anytime.

But, as always, there are limits. "When the 'star word' is used, I squirm," says Scott Pioli, the general manager of the Kansas City Chiefs. Scott had a big hand in assembling the New England Patriots football teams that went to four Super Bowls, so he knows a little something about supervising the high-strung and talented. Do you treat your stars differently? Pioli has very strict guidelines for that. Compensation is an easy one. Most everyone understands that some folks make more than others based on how well they do on the job. But that's where the star treatment ends for Pioli. There are basic rules everyone has to follow. "You don't want to create an obnoxiously apparent class system," Pioli explains. "Everything else has to be consistent in terms of rules.

"There are certain core things everyone has to abide by," he continues. "Working hard, being on time . . . those are things you can't compromise."

Keeping the Talent in Check

Sometimes, you do need to be tough on your "A" players, and knowing when to do so can be a bit tricky. While you have to treat your stars well, you can't just let them walk over you. My son is a talented lacrosse player/goalie and he knows he is. I was having a discussion with one of his coaches, asking him to threaten to suspend my son for a game if he didn't do his homework. "We don't want to do that," said the coach. "We need him." Oh, okay. (Don't they always say school is supposed to come first?) How about kicking him out of a practice or two? He loves practices, believe it or not. No, said the coach. We need him for practice, too.

You can end up in the same no-man's-land with your stars. Basically, you have to call them on outrageous conduct. A *Boston Globe* columnist once refused to make the changes I asked him to make in a piece. I said, "Okay, have it your way. I'm killing your column." No one ever killed his column before. Much less touched his copy. He was so shocked he agreed to make the changes. Another talented guy, who was bordering on insubordinate, would mention the name of an executive on the corporate masthead as if that would help him get his way. (This is the worst. Never, ever tolerate name checking. If you have to quit, do just that if it continues.) I had to explain to him (read: yell at him) that I will make decisions regardless of what his supposed friend in high places thinks. In other words: no one is above the law. Scott Pioli of the Chiefs basically says you have to pick your poison. Whatever you do to make your stars happy, you have to do it in the open, not hide it for the sake of protecting the egos of your less-standout employees. More money? The Bill Russell treatment? All in the open. "If you try and mask it," says Pioli, "it affects credibility."

A Different Way to Think About Hiring

When I first called Jim Collins, famous for his book *Good to Great,* our topic was supposed to be crisis management. But as it turned out, the conversation veered into the importance of hiring the *right* people (partly because Jim hasn't done research in that topic during his studies of the world's great companies—and he never writes anything without research). Hiring *right* means finding folks who aren't just talented, but also fit your needs, some of which can't be anticipated. I never quite thought about it this way. As Jim points out, good leaders have no way to predict the future. They have no way of knowing what situations might come up. But, says Collins, you "have to prepare for what (you) can't predict."

If you know Collins, you know he loves rock climbing. So any conversation with him will eventually get you there. It's a metaphor for everything and anything "Collins." And it scares me to say this—partly because I'm not a fan of such management philosophies—it makes sense. Jim had a friend who was climbing the Emperor Face on Mount Robson in the Canadian Rockies. The climb hadn't been repeated for thirty years. He asked his friend: "Because no one had been on it (in recent years) you didn't know what the mountain was going to throw at you. Ice, snow, loose rock. But the mountain face was so big that there was no coming down. How did you prepare?" His friend said: "I understood that the single most important preparation was picking my partner . . . I looked at our skill set . . . between the two of us, we should be able to deal with whatever the mountain throws at us."

There are a lot of things, as Collins says, that go into "business genius." But the "genius for picking the right person for the right activity" is about near the top. A lot of it has to do with knowing what type of skills you're going to need down the road. To be sure, a lot of that isn't knowable. It's basically having people who have the talent to deal with "whatever comes up." Says Collins: "I don't know what it is like in the desert, but I have to have someone who is good in the desert."

It's true. In my business, you don't know what kind of stories you're going to tackle. But you know you're going to have to write stories that require writers who have the ability to confront powerful forces in government or business or both. You need journalists who are tough-minded and don't shy away from confrontation. One of the smartest personnel moves I've seen a guy make was when my boss, Andy Serwer, was looking for someone to run *Fortune*'s Web site. He didn't know everything that person would have to deal with, but he knew he needed someone who had both the journalistic fingertips as well as a feel for just about anything digital. We came up with Daniel Roth, a *Wired* magazine writer/editor who was previously at *Fortune*. He was young, but not too young. He knew the digital landscape. He was, at one point, an editor at *Fortune*. More important, he was a journalist who understood *Fortune*'s core: smart analysis and deeply reported narrative writing. As soon as he was hired, *Fortune* decided to produce an edition that could be downloaded on Apple's new iPad. We had the right guy—Dan Roth. Hell, Andy didn't know we'd be producing an edition of *Fortune* for the iPad. But he knew he needed someone who had both digital skills and *Fortune*'s DNA. Andy didn't know what was going to happen in the desert, but he knew the guy who could deal with it.

Who's Got Talent?

Hiring stars, in real life, is relatively simple. They have a track record—an extensive body of work, in other words—and often a lot of industry awards. It's hard to go terribly wrong if you really do your homework. And if you have "New York Yankee money" to dole out, no problem. But figuring out who on your staff, especially your younger employees, has those rare intangibles is a whole other matter. You often just overlook skills someone might have. Back at *The Wall Street Journal,* I was looking for a transfer to the Boston bureau. My mother wasn't well and I wanted to move closer to home. There were no openings, so I took a job at *The Boston Globe,* where I eventually became a successful editor. Years later, I was visiting with Norm Pearlstine, the editor-in-chief of Time Inc., who was editor of *The Wall Street Journal* when I left for the *Globe*. The first thing he said to me was something like, "I'm sorry I didn't figure out you had talent as an editor when you were at the *Journal*." I said, "How were you supposed to know?"

It was a good question, I think.

It's extremely difficult to discover the stars of the future on your own staff. Who among your rookies will climb the mountain with you? Will they, as Jim Collins might say, learn enough to survive there? You usually know the good writers right off the bat. They can turn a phrase. They know what a topic sentence is. They can figure out how to explain the point of the story early in the piece. They're usually pretty smart, too. We have one writer at *Fortune* who becomes an instant expert before she starts reporting a story. One of her editors told me that, prior to starting an investing piece, she actually read two or three books on the subject. You know you have a winner when they do that.

But discovering talent is pretty much like drafting NFL players. Until they start blocking and tackling in real games, you just don't know what you have. I had one bright writer who on paper looked great. Ivy League graduate, hard worker, good researcher. But she'd always beg off stories when things got tough. The projects with a high degree of difficulty *always* failed. Bad signs. I had other smart writers who took months to turn in stories. There was always an excuse. ("I had work to do for the issue we just finished. . . .") Others complain they don't know what kind of ideas the editors like—a really lame excuse for not coming up with ideas your boss likes, by the way. And yet, we somehow, at the same time, employed a rookie reporter who had an incredible knack for coming up with ideas and getting feature stories in the magazine. He never asked what kinds of stories I liked. He just pitched ideas, and more often than not I'd say, go do it! (He was a bit challenged accuracy-wise, but never mind.)

And sometimes you don't know for a while. One reporter, an intern, was a surefire major leaguer. He could write. He could think. He could report difficult and arcane topics and put them in English. I would have put money down that he'd be a star. But years later, I was having a discussion about him with another editor. I couldn't understand why he never rose to the next level. My friend, the editor, got it right in about two words: "He's boring." And he was right. He was boring. His ideas were boring, his writing, though clear, rarely came alive, and it didn't help that he was slow. I somehow missed the boring factor. Those darn intangibles.

So what do you do? Well, in the case of the boring guy, you just move on. If you're thinking about why someone doesn't really get better, it's time to let go. You can't do much about "boring." I can already tell with some of our younger staffers who struggle. If you have a tough story, you just turn to someone else. If you have a soft, easy task, you turn to them. But look for clues early. The person who reads a slew of books to learn the topic inside out; the person who studies a year's worth of stories before starting reporting; the writer who likes to knock on doors instead of just dealing with public relations folks; the writer who is not afraid of a good confrontation. Then, all things being equal, you've got something special.

But perhaps the toughest job is taking someone talented and making them better. I always thought that's what made Los Angeles Lakers coach Phil Jackson so great. He's won eleven championships in the National Basketball Association with the Lakers and the Chicago Bulls. His critics like to say he always lands on teams with the likes of Michael Jordan and Kobe Bryant. But what he does better than anyone is make star players better, taking them to the next level within a team concept. Jordan didn't win any championships before Jackson came along, and Bryant didn't win a title without Shaquille O'Neal before Jackson came along. I'm sure each would have gotten there, but I'm also sure they wouldn't have won as many championships without Jackson. (By the way, I just hate to admit that, being part of the Celtics/Red Auerbach fan club. To us, Jackson's the Antichrist.)

Some of my more rewarding experiences as a manager have been taking stars and making them better. I worked with Jane Bryant Quinn at *Newsweek* during the nineties. She is, and was, the Michael Jordan of personal finance reporting. Jane didn't need my help writing columns. Or thinking. Or reporting. All I did was help her choose the right stories to do. Jane had never won the Gerald Loeb Award for business journalism, one of the profession's top prizes. I solved that problem by asking Jane to focus on covering insurance salespeople who unnecessarily encouraged their customers to change policies. She liked doing those kinds of hard-hitting stories. But no one actively encouraged her. I asked her to do those types of stories all the time.

But if I had a "greatest hit," it might be my work with Andy Serwer, *Fortune*'s top editor now, when he was a writer. In the late nineties, my lunch companion had just stood me up at the now-defunct Judson Grill. At another table were Joe Nocera (of *Fortune* and now a *New York Times* columnist), Andy, and Bob Safian, also of *Fortune* and now editor of *Fast Company* magazine. They invited me to join them. I knew Andy a bit—I hadn't been at *Fortune* that long—but I didn't know him in this setting. I was stunned. You could tell he would eventually be a star, even though he wasn't at the time. It must have been what it was like when Brian Epstein heard the Beatles for the first time. (Well, not exactly like that, but close enough.) He was rapping a mile a minute about the business stories of the day. He was also hilariously funny. And, most of all, he knew what he was talking about. I always wanted to produce a business column that included the best elements of sports writing. You know—funny, smart, lots of attitude and opinion. It just wasn't done much, if at all, back in those days. (God forbid you should make fun of corporate executives. They're so sensitive.)

Andy was my guy. I decided that during the lunch. He had a sports column trapped inside him. I spent the next few days trying to convince John Huey, *Fortune*'s boss, to let Andy write a Web column. Since it was on the Web, I figured no one would care if we screwed up or went over the top. No one cared much about what you posted on the Web back then. (I'm not sure anyone cares now either; maybe a little. It's getting better.) It was Shangri-la for anyone who wanted to do anything different. We could do it any way we liked. Say whatever we liked. Markets, basketball, CEOs who were doing stupid things. Rock and roll. Anything, really.

So Andy did just that. We called it "Street Life," after a song by the progressive rock band Roxy Music. (Get it? Life on Wall Street?) I told Andy to write like a gonzo sports columnist. That was all you needed to tell him. That was my only contribution. And the column became a Web cult hit of sorts. Andy also became a megastar *Fortune* writer as a result. *The New Yorker* wrote about the column: they called Andy the stock market's "own poet-singer." (Not sure exactly what they meant, but it sounded good.) He also got a great TV gig on CNN out of it.

Just call me Phil.

The Cardinal Sins of Hiring

(AND THE DUMB THINGS YOU DO RIGHT AFTER)

☛ There are a slew of things you can do to screw up as a manager. I know because I've done just about all of them. I haven't given enough feedback, or at least honest feedback. I've picked the wrong people to produce the right stories. I keep making some of the same mistakes over and over again—ask anyone who has worked for me—though not as often after all these years in the business.

How bad can it get if you have no idea what you're doing? Here's a little role-playing scenario: Pretend you're a general manager of a pro basketball team. You've just taken a really bad first-round draft pick in the NBA draft. Here's how many things can go wrong. First off, you've spent a lot of money signing the guy. You wasted a lot of time vetting him—doing a lousy job at that to boot. Then, once it all goes bad, all the other players on the team resent the fact that the new rich guy, just out of high school probably, spends more time with his Bloomberg terminal checking on his investments than setting picks. (He has his contract. He's rich. Why should he work hard?) Of course, you keep the guy longer than you should. You figure he might get it if you wait long enough and besides you're afraid you'll look bad because you made such a stupid decision. Not only that, you'll give him tasks he's not capable of executing, again, because you want to justify your own brilliant choice. Meanwhile, it puts a strain on the whole organization—somebody has got to do the work—until you finally cut him from the team and start all over again. To be sure, you never admit your mistake!

So, from a management point of view, you've done a lot of things wrong here. Maybe set a record. You did a lousy job of vetting and you overlooked the advice of a former coach who told you that this player tended to coast when he felt too secure and comfortable. And you compounded the problem by not cutting the player quickly. You played him at the expense of the team in hopes it would eventually work out. Everyone in your organization resents you because you screwed up so badly and never explained yourself. In fact, you probably blamed some hapless scout for the whole mess, because that's what some managers do when things go wrong.

All these mistakes happen in real life. Sometimes it all plays out like this, when everything goes wrong at once. More likely you're doing some of the above some of the time. The following is a list of some of the really foolish things you can do, and a little advice on how to avoid these problems. There's no particular ranking. It's all bad. Call them my "Hiring Sins." I could give you about a hundred of them, but these just seem to come up over and over again.

• SIN #1 •

Hiring Someone Because Someone Else Says You Should

If I were running one of those aspirational management seminars, I'd show everyone season three of *Curb Your Enthusiasm.* Larry David, Ted Danson, and Michael York are partners in a trendy L.A. restaurant. They spend months trying to hire the right chef. There are the usual Larry David cringe-worthy moments. For instance, when he tries out a chef who, at a dinner party, makes a meal with peanuts and practically poisons Richard Lewis's allergy-plagued girlfriend, who refuses to take Benadryl because she's a Christian Scientist. (Follow that?) They finally find the right guy to cook, on the recommendation of a nasty food critic, and eventually discover that he has Tourette's syndrome. A detail, by the way, they chose to ignore. Anyway, on opening night, there he is standing in the open kitchen yelling out "FUCK" for all the customers to hear.

Pretty funny, but it also makes a good point. I'm not picking on anyone here, but we all hire people on appearances and take credentials at face value. Especially when we're in a rush. Really, who among you spends a whole lot of time vetting potential employees? You ask around, get a headhunter, get a few recommendations, and pretend you can trust LinkedIn. You're so happy you have a budget to hire anyone at all that you'd grab the first warm body walking down the street. In my field, it's sometimes as simple as "Bob won a big prize so he must be great." That would seem to be a no-brainer, don't you think? But consider a few things. First, Bob may have won his prize as part of a team. You know, someone else did the real work.

You know, the guy sitting on the bench watching Laker teammate Kobe Bryant lay fifty points on the Celtics and waving his towel. He'll get his championship ring, but he didn't do much to earn it. So what do you do? You have to personally check the work. You can't fake good ideas and you can't fake good thinking.

Try to reach mid-level people who have seen the employee's raw work. I only give referrals when I think I can be 100 percent enthusiastic because the person is actually worth a great referral. And that's what I look for when I'm on the other end and find myself asking others what they think of someone. If the recommendation is "I kinda liked the guy," run the other way. It's got to be an over-the-top "I love the guy" before I'll even take one seriously. That is just a hard-and-fast rule. Don't ever deviate from it.

A quick aside: Although you should only give (and take) recommendations you really believe in, that doesn't mean you should slam someone you're not all that enthusiastic about. First of all, you can get your ass sued off if your reference becomes the job killer. And even if you are honest, the bad referral, honest to God, can come back to haunt you. Good referrals mean friends for life; bad ones mean you'd better start sleeping with one eye open. A number of years ago I was asked for a reference about one of my writers. Dick, as I'll call him, was supersmart and a terrific writer. I told the *Washington Post* editor who called that he was a slightly lazy reporter and could be, at times, a bit passive-aggressive (translation: a disruptive prick). I also said he was potentially a great talent. Well, within days, Dick was in my office repeating my "recommendation" word for word. "Why'd you say these things about me?" (I can't clearly recall my response to that, but it was something like "Somebody else must have said that.There are a lot of people here who don't like you." The last part was true, anyway.) He got the job, but it turned out to be a mess, because I was honest. The jerk editor from *The Washington Post* broke the cardinal rule of referrals: don't tell the job candidate exactly where the negative stuff is coming from.

I've changed a few habits these days, especially when dealing with job candidates who aren't all that perfect. I tell you this only because you're going to run into people like me all the time: people who won't tell the whole truth about a job candidate because they don't like spending time in depositions. For example, I got a call a few years back from a newspaper editor looking for a copywriter who had once worked for me. The guy was okay if you didn't have anyone else around at the time to do the work. (Hiring him was kind of like eating at a Denny's when you're driving cross-country. The alternative is Cracker Barrel, so you just go along with it.) But he would be my last choice for any major project. In fact, I was going to fire him. Here's how it went:

> EDITOR: Hi, Hank, my name is Bob Jones. Tom had your name down as a reference (the guy must have been really desperate, I thought). Can you tell me a little bit about him? (Note: Don't start out with a question like that; cut to the chase—"Is this guy any good?")

> ME: Hi, Bob. I would really like to help you, but I have a policy that I don't give references. You know, the HR folks are really afraid that an honest review will come back to bite us in the ass. (Yup, that was his big clue. He didn't jump on it. I tried. Not my problem.)

EDITOR: Sorry about that, Hank. Maybe next time.

ME: Well, I'm sorry, too. Tell Tom I said hello, good luck, and that we miss him. (Now, that's true, I did miss him. He was a great guy to talk sports with.)

Now, poor old Bob Jones thinks there's something positive about the guy without my actually giving him a stamp of approval. That's what you're up against. But I wasn't particularly proud of that moment. I guess I was so guilty about firing the guy. And I really did like talking about sports with him.

So how do you get around all this? I'm a believer in scout teams: friends and former colleagues who work at other companies and will just tell you the truth. If you have worked at a lot of places, like I have, you have a lot of friends. It's the only way to get honest feedback—ever. They've seen the person's work firsthand and even know his or her bosses. They either warn you off or enthusiastically give you a thumbs-up. It can work a couple of ways. Before we hired James Bandler from *The Wall Street Journal*, I knew him only from his work as part of a Pulitzer Prize–winning team that produced the stories that triggered the stock option backdating scandals a few years back. James was initially recommended by Dan Okrent, one of the smartest journalist/authors around (and one of the inventors of Rotisserie baseball, for those of you interested in such things). I wanted to make sure he wasn't Kobe Bryant's towel-waver. Dan said he was available and we should hire James if we had the vacancy and the money. I turned to friends in Boston who said I should hire him, maybe in the next five minutes. I read all his work, obviously. But that's the kind of recommendation you need. Saved us a lot of time.

✖

On another occasion, I was asked to vet a writer from an important newspaper who had a pretty good reputation. Fortunately, my network included many writers and editors where she worked. The verdict: nice person, works hard but doesn't break a sweat, and her stories don't make much of an impact. Got the *exact* same story every time. We hired her anyway and the book on her couldn't have been more accurate. Very productive, *nice,* but left no footprints. (In my business, that means no impact. In Jack Welch's General Electric land, that means a C-plus player. Maybe less because Jack was known for being kind of a mean manager.)

Sometimes your scout team gives you reports before you even think about hiring. One day I was meeting a writer for lunch when out of the blue he told me he had heard a former colleague might apply for a job at my publication. I won't bore you with the details, but he told me to not even think about hiring this guy. A petty, backbiting, mean, self-promoting idiot. Whew! And this was a guy with a pretty good reputation. As it turned out, we actually thought about hiring him at one point. Thank goodness for the scout team.

Now, sometimes employees don't work out at a former employer for a number of reasons. I hired a freelancer who didn't cut it, apparently, at *The New York Times*. My scout team explained why. He left the *Times* because he didn't get along with his boss, who wasn't particularly sharp. The take: he had a lot of upside and was capable of doing very difficult stories. Sometimes you have to bet on upside, you just do. (And those types of people are bargains.) But, hell, there's no way of knowing that unless you do the right kind of vetting. And don't think you've done your job if you pay a headhunter to do it for you. That's exactly what I would do at some point in my career: hire a headhunter and figure they're responsible for making sure I don't screw up. A year or so ago a headhunter called me about a job candidate I was familiar with and asked me what I'd "heard about them." He was clearly hoping I had heard something good. Anything good. (The guy was kind to cab drivers and stray cats, whatever.) That's how much the headhunter, I'll call him "Steve," wanted to send this guy to his client and wrap up the search. My first thought: Steve does this for a living—how could he not know the candidate was disliked by his employees, was a pathological micromanager, and had been quietly sent to the penalty box on a sterile corporate floor. Sometimes you don't want to know. But somebody should.

• SIN #2 •

Falling in Love with Job Applicants

Once upon a time, an employee at a national publication was considering me for a senior editor's job. I was an obscure journalist at a local newspaper at the time and pretty excited about the prospect of working for what was, believe it or not, readers, a pretty hot national magazine. But I found out soon enough that I wasn't the top candidate. What the publication's editors didn't know was that *I* knew. Their top choice was a former colleague, if you were wondering how I figured this out. I also knew she wasn't right for the job. The woman was a great talent but did not like managing people. Can you believe that? But they were in love with her because, among other things, she had what I call "badge cred." In other words: she worked for a famous brand-name publication. They loved the woman so much that they sent her champagne. But, what the hell. Even though I knew I wasn't a top pick, I was always up for a trip to New York and wanted to see what someone from that publication actually looked like.

I was called down to New York for an interview at the bar at the Helmsley Hotel, which looked like a place really old couples would go to have affairs if they had enough energy. I could tell right away that the two guys grilling me wanted to be anywhere else but with me. The first "let's get this over with" question was "What kind of magazines do you read?" We peaked there. (If you are ever asked that question during a job interview, end the whole thing right there. Just a bit of advice.) Number One, after five minutes, said he had to go, leaving me with Number Two, who seemed like he wanted to go out the door with Number One. He did, about ten minutes later. We walked out, and a car service was waiting for him. (They had this worked out to the minute!) I was left fending for myself at rush hour in New York City, trying to get a cab to the airport. I guess the message was "We like this other person so we have no reason to be polite. Have a nice life."

When I got back home, I called Number Two's assistant and asked for my writing and editing samples back. They never sent them. Months later, Number Two called and asked me back to New York for another round of interviews. The woman they lusted after had clearly turned them down and now, after actually looking at my work, they wanted to talk more. I eventually got the job, but they took a big risk focusing on one person for so long. They could have chosen a woman who was neither a great manager nor a skilled magazine maker at the expense of someone, me, who was pretty decent at both things. It's like buying a house—don't fall in love with it, and be prepared to walk away if it costs too much. I never did get champagne like the candidate they really wanted. But I'm not bitter. Well, I am, to tell you the truth.

This brings me to another important point. A lot of mistakes are made in hiring because people love to go by appearances. It's the courtship thing all over again. He/she is good-looking and everything he/she says is smart and funny because, well, he/she is mighty attractive. But when you reach the 352-day mark, the illusion vanishes. Then it's too late. You're stuck with him or her for a while and, maybe, headed for a painful breakup. Hiring is like that as well.

Appearances can mean a lot of things. It's the "badge cred" phenomenon, like I said before. One boss I knew loved to hire from *The Wall Street Journal* because it looked good to his bosses. It didn't matter that he had a lot of better people in his own stable to promote. His bosses would be impressed that he had been able to hire someone away from *The Wall Street Journal* so it didn't matter. It was easy: he wouldn't have to explain himself like he would if he picked someone they were already familiar with or who was from a lesser publication. It was like the old days with IBM and in-house tech guys. You couldn't get fired if you brought in someone from IBM. You could get fired if you hired someone from a smaller, less well-known company and it didn't work out.

Of course, appearances can actually matter. Let's go back to Number One and Number Two again. There were a number of reasons they didn't like me at first. I wore a suit that looked like I just bought it from JCPenney for the interview. They wore Armani. I was short, they were super tall. I talked in a

Boston accent, they talked like they just walked out of a school that specialized in prep school accents. You can miss out on a lot of good people by judging them this way. (Not bitter . . .) There's no reason to overlook talent by only hiring people who walk, talk, and dress just like you, or have worked at *The Wall Street Journal*. Which I did, by the way. But even that couldn't overcome my stint at the local paper and the bad suit.

• SIN #3 •
Casting the Right People for the Wrong Job

After all these years as an editor, I still make this mistake, sometimes, but I try not to. If you can rid yourself of one of these management sins, this would be the one. You hire someone new and then give them a task they're not suited to. It's the "asking the short guy to dunk the basketball" thing. It makes no sense. Yet we do it time and time again.

Everybody likes the big assignment. The tough story, the challenging sales call, the complex research project. But the very worst thing you can do for anyone is put them in a position where they're sure to fail. In the baseball playoffs of 2003, then Red Sox manager Grady Little left star pitcher Pedro Martinez in the game for an extra inning because of some sense of loyalty to the guy (or at least it seemed that way). Let him be the hero! It all blew up. Martinez was clearly out of gas. The Yankees just killed him, and Red Sox fans everywhere were about to drink the poisoned Kool-Aid. That's what I'm talking about.

✖

Now, I know what you're going to say: you don't really know about someone until you give them a chance. Well, actually, that's totally wrong. You do know. Your gut tells you. You know what your employees can do or cannot do after the very first tasks they do for you. It's why you start people out with a number of smaller assignments. You know if they can work under pressure or can't work under pressure. You know if they are solid reporters but better storytellers. You know all this. And if you don't, you find out soon enough.

There are a number of different ways this can go right and wrong. Early in 2009 my boss, Andy Serwer, and I had a number of conversations about how we could get in on the Bernie Madoff scam story. It wasn't as easy as you might think. We were pretty much outflanked by armies of reporters from the likes of *The Wall Street Journal* and *The New York Times*. What could we bring to the party? We decided we'd just have to dive in with a small team and see what we could dig up. It was a big investment in time, money, and resources for a small staff of writers and reporters (uh, at the time). We'd essentially have to take two of our best writers and our best researcher and devote up to half a year to get this done. There was a big risk of failure.

So the casting was crucial. The first writer we picked was James Bandler. We needed someone who was a master reporter, who was comfortable dealing with documents, talking to prosecutors, and courting defense lawyers, and who didn't discourage easily. Other writers, facing reluctant sources and skilled competitors, wilt under the pressure. They're afraid. James wasn't afraid. He was Kobe Bryant with the ball in his hands with ten seconds left in the game. That was the easy part. Picking a partner for James was harder. The skill set had to be somewhat the same, but the partner's talents had to add something. We picked Nick Varchaver. Nick was deliberate, a great thinker, very careful, and a terrific editor to boot. Believe it or not, we had to think about how the process would be at the end. You never know, even after months of work, how quickly you have to publish if the competition is heating up. Nick was a first-rate writer who would help produce a strong draft for the primary editor, Tim Smith.

He would also be a de facto editor during the whole process. He'd ask all the questions editors ask, but during the research stage itself. We added our all-star researcher Doris Burke, who was a whiz records expert and consistently dug up original material. (Doris worked on the Enron masterpiece: the book, *The Smartest Guys in the Room* with Bethany McLean, Joe Nocera, and Peter Elkind.) Everyone had their role and their skills meshed.

We eventually produced a twenty-plus-page article that was not only an incredible example of storytelling, but broke news (and also went on to win a few awards). This would never have worked if we didn't get the casting just right. I can't pretend we planned all this. But we did know exactly who wouldn't be good for the job. There were no assurances that the team was going to produce. But what we did know was that they were capable of producing, and we knew we had nailed the casting part. If we failed, it wouldn't be because the managers screwed up choosing the players.

The worst casting mistake you can make is giving an assignment to someone because you want to give them a chance or because you like them, or both. (See Grady Little and Pedro

Martinez.) This happens a lot, especially with new hires. It's natural to want to help out folks who you brought on and give them plum assignments. But you're not doing them any favors if you give them a task they're not just right for.

Now, sometimes the choice seems obvious and still backfires. I once had an economics writer who knew about everything there was to know about how the economy functioned. We had a big piece to produce on the direction of the U.S. economy—and we had to do it quickly and in a colorful way. I lobbied for this writer and he dived into the project. But the final result was dull and academic. The editor-in-chief thought less of the writer and thought less of me for not going with someone who was a better storyteller. It didn't matter that this guy was an expert. Readers would stop reading after a couple of sentences. Here are the things that went wrong. First, I shouldn't have been so stubborn. I knew that my bosses didn't like this writer. Some of it was personal and just plain stupid. But some of it was absolutely right. He was dull; not "pop" enough. I knew this and ignored it because he was my guy. I wanted to show my bosses who was boss. In any event, I shouldn't have fought this battle under such a tight deadline. He was also the wrong guy for the task. I knew he wasn't a slick writer. He could take complex ideas and make them very clear, but without flair. If a writer could clear the room, he was that writer. (Not because he couldn't do it, he just didn't think taking serious subjects and putting lipstick on them was dignified. And I say this in a complimentary way!)

Deep down inside, I knew this was going to be trouble. And it was. It was trouble for the writer because he had to rewrite the piece. It was trouble for me because I had to spend more time editing the piece. (Not to mention my bosses thought I was an idiot for even giving the guy the project.) It was trouble for our copydesk because they had to rush the rewrite through to meet deadlines. It was trouble for everyone because I was trying to make someone happy. I didn't serve anyone well because I didn't want to hurt someone's feelings. I was stubborn and ignored the obvious. I would have fired *me.*

• SIN #4 •
Not Giving Feedback

I can hardly recall the last time I ever told a writer he did a lousy job. I can vividly recall the one time an editor told me I screwed up. It was back in the 1980s while I was at *The Wall Street Journal.* One of my favorite bosses ever, Kathy Christensen, said to me at dinner: "Your first front-page piece was terrific. Your last one really sucked." Or something like that. (And she laughed when she said it. She was a riot.) It was a shock, to be sure. But she was right and I knew it. So I spent the next couple of days figuring out what I did wrong. It wasn't pleasant. Kind of like going cold turkey to break a narcotics habit, not that I know anything about that. But Kathy's critique did the trick and I didn't make the same mistakes again.

Bosses rarely offer up honest feedback. And employees, like me at that time, are totally shocked when they do. As I write this, I haven't had a formal performance evaluation at Time Inc. in the fourteen years I've been here. (I get raises, so I figure I must be doing something right. Maybe that's better.) It happens like this everywhere I've worked.

One time I was talking with one of my veteran writers and he asked me what I thought of his most recent story. "Well," I said, doing the best Kathy Christensen imitation I could muster, "it wasn't your best. It could have been better written and the reporting wasn't all that surprising. Better luck next time." He walked away, with just an "okay" in response. But he looked like he'd just had a heart attack. I heard from other editors for a couple of days about how he was thrown for a loop because I actually doled out some live feedback. He couldn't stop talking about it. It was kind of funny, but it didn't say anything positive about us as managers. Me, in particular. In other words, when it came to telling people what they needed to know about their work, we were absolutely pathetic.

The problem is most managers are afraid of giving honest feedback. And it's easy to understand why. I mean, the point of being a boss is to order people around, be the center of attention, and dole out good news like raises—right? Who wants to deliver bad news? We're all chicken. Still, the no-feedback loop causes all sorts of unintended problems. First, when you're trying to fire someone—and you've never told them they were doing a lousy job—it comes as, usually, a total surprise. Sometimes you have to wonder how they could have overlooked the warning signs. I've had employees express shock when they haven't been in print or online for months. (Them: "You never gave me any feedback." Me: "Well, we never publish your stories—enough feedback for you?") But still, you have to tell people how they're doing. Even if you think they should know how they're doing.

Not all feedback has to be nasty. Tell them what kind of projects they can be working on and what kind of things not to work on. The best piece of advice I got was from an editor at

The Wall Street Journal. I told her I wanted to write one of those quirky front-page stories—you know, the ones on toilet testing labs and suicide rates at wineries in Finland. (I wrote the one about toilet testing labs. Look it up!) She said—actually she snarled—that my time would be better spent on stories that were serious and could actually result in raises for me. That sank in. It allowed me for years to work on the right kind of stories. Or at least think about it the right way. (Though the "raise" part never quite worked out.)

The Wall Street Journal circa 1984 was great for all sorts of good advice I'd carry forward, even as a manager. It's twenty-five-plus years down the road, but I still remember how an editor told me that the best stories were the risky ones, the stories with the highest odds of failure. You ever work with people who love grinding out projects that are neither bad nor great? Just smack in the middle? There's no point in that. Might as well be bad, and move on to another career, than be mediocre. Another time I was struggling with a story during the editing process. It was a complicated piece on textile quotas (don't ask me what I was doing writing that). I just couldn't write about it in a clear way. I couldn't understand it myself. As it turns out, neither did my editor. My boss for that story, cut to the chase. "Usually, when you have so much trouble writing something it means you didn't do enough reporting or you did the wrong kind of reporting," she said. She not only gave me some advice that would help me write and edit for years, but told me the truth about how I was doing my job. In other words: at least for that story, I stunk. And it was okay. In fact, it was great. I knew there was something wrong with the piece, but had no clue what the problem was. I was working hard, but was working hard on the wrong things. And she was tough-minded enough to tell me. Other editors would just ask a few questions and do it themselves.

You can, of course, go too far. There are those who think that the Bobby Knight rule of management is the way to go—the ones who get in your face and tell you "you're a worthless piece of you know what and maybe you should die." I was once writing about a guy named Olin King. Olin was founder of a company called SCI Systems in Huntsville, Alabama, which made, among other things, circuit boards for PCs. I think he was the meanest manager I ever met. He would describe to me how he would put his face inches from the face of his employees before he gave them a tongue-lashing. The effect was better that way. All that was missing was the chain saw. He was proud of being a bully. Here's how King put it: "Sometimes you get the facts better by arguing with people . . . you can spend half the day going back and forth with an employee or you can say, 'Why are you lying to me?' You get to the core of it that way." (Olin King also provided me with one of the best quotes ever when he described how important his business and working were to him: "I've had one company and two wives," he told me. "And that ought to tell you something.")

He also liked to be sneaky. For instance, he smoked out bad managers during the company picnic by setting up a dunking booth. As it turned out, the most unpopular managers were also picked for dunking booth duty. Got dunking booth duty? You were a dead man to Olin. That was your feedback. No way anyone was going to enjoy anything—ever. You had to be on your toes, and really paranoid, to survive working for Mr. Olin King.

I never found this strategy particularly effective. For one thing, I couldn't pull it off. (Look at my picture on the jacket of this book: Is this a scary face? Please don't answer that.) It's the wrong kind of feedback. You sure as hell get rid of less talented folks, but at the same time the good ones head for the hills, too, eventually. There was a reason Bobby Knight, the basketball coach at Indiana University for years, became an ineffective recruiter at one point. The kids just didn't like an old guy in their face. (Olin King? After I wrote about him and his company, the dunking booth trick was exposed and he couldn't use it anymore. Saving southern middle managers one man at a time!)

• SIN #5 •
Hiring People with Severe Personality Disorders as Managers

To this day, I'm stunned by shy folks who go into management. It's kind of the fault of the system. If you pay people more for being in management, everyone is eventually going to want to do it. But jeez, a lot of these folks just seem to hate people and any kind of human interaction. I remember an interview I had with a young man at the time for a position at *Fortune* that had just opened up. He was in no way management material. Not because he wasn't smart. He just hated most people. He had no respect for his coworkers, who, by the way, he would have to manage. I asked him why in hell he wanted to run the department. His response: "The pay is a lot better." An honest answer. But not the right answer. A lot of people would have given him the job anyway because he had so much talent. The result?

They'd lose him in a job he was great at—and probably lose some folks who would be forced to work for the new, and surly, boss.

There are other people, though, who just pass by and become managers because someone either likes them or owes them a favor or it is the only way to give someone very talented a significant promotion. How else could you even explain the guy I'm about to describe to you?

I was on a job interview a number of years ago. It was at a restaurant in New York where media types—when they thought they were Wall Street types—would take people out for dinner. I was, for some reason, becoming pretty animated about a few things I was really good at, such as generating story ideas. "I really love talking about story ideas," I recall saying to my dinner partner, who was interviewing me for a job. "Do you?" There was a few seconds' pause. No smile from my dinner partner. I was waiting for the answer. It had to be "Yes." Right? "No," he finally said. "Not really." Okay, I thought. I guess I can live with that if I get the job. As long as I know. Well, that was really weird. That was the first time in my career, in what I think we'd all agree is a creative business, that someone said they didn't like talking about ideas. It's like playing baseball and not liking to play catch.

I thought of this a few years later. Bosses, at least many of them, don't like to talk with their employees. I haven't figured it out other than to say that a lot of shy folks go into the business and a lot just like to spend their time talking with *their* bosses. A full-time job in itself. (It's called "managing up," if you were wondering.) A pal of mine once went to see the same guy and actually had the nerve to walk into his office and talk about a story he was working on. A few minutes later, he was called back into the office. The conversation went something like this: "Don't you ever come into my office again and talk about story ideas." I will swear on any Bible that this is a *true* story. My friend was a little confused. After all, the whole business is built around story ideas. It's what we do. But our mutual boss just liked to be alone, deal with e-mail, and expense really expensive meals with *his* work friends.

• SIN #6 •
Cheating Your Employees

There are a lot of bosses out there who do stupid things. But one of the very worst is cheating your employees. You know, don't give someone a raise because your bottom line will look better and your bonus will be higher. You nickel and dime them with expenses. You don't pay them market rates. As a result of that, they probably aren't particularly loyal, and so they eventually leave. And if they don't leave, there is a lot of bad blood.

I first learned that the hard way back in 1973. My dad had owned a business that cleaned movie theaters and supermarkets. (You ever wonder who swept all that popcorn off the theater floor? Cleaned those soda-soaked floors? He did. I did.) Dad died in 1973 and I was stuck trying to run his business as a twenty-year-old who didn't know a damn thing. One day, I had forgotten to pay an employee what was exactly due him. Now, you have to know these were not your usual white-collar guys. Some had guns in the trunks of their cars. Some had scars from razor blade fights. Some were minor-league drug dealers. Well, I assumed they were just minor league. Anyway, this guy called me up and said, in so many words, "I know where you live so don't cheat me."

Good lesson. They always know where you live. (Yes, I paid him.)

You just can't win with this stuff. I'm not asking for an audit or anything, but picky bean counters just don't save all that much money. I get constant complaints from my employees about auditors in Bangalore (at least I think that's where they are) nitpicking their expenses. (Thanks, McKinsey. How much did we pay you for that idea?) Here's an old story, probably apocryphal, that shows you what really happens. Apparently, a veteran *Time* magazine reporter had bought an expensive winter coat for an assignment in the Arctic. He expensed the coat and was rejected. The next time he submitted expenses, he called his business manager. "Try," he said, "to find the coat."

Salaries are a big issue, too, and they're fraught with danger. If you pay too little, you can lose an employee to another competitor; if you pay too much, you can offend your equally deserving employees who are paid less. (Trust me, all employees eventually find out what their peers are making.) People are always worried that someone else is paid more than they are. They're always thinking about making more money elsewhere. I had a friend at *The Wall Street Journal* in the eighties. He was a great reporter, a book author, and won a Pulitzer. He was never happy with his salary. Finally, he got a very rich offer from *Newsweek*. He took the offer and went back to our boss, who said he'd match it. Without any hesitation my friend said, "Why didn't you just pay me when I asked for a raise years ago?" "Because," our boss answered, "I didn't know what you were worth."

Can't argue with that. But it did force my pal to look for a job, and the *Journal* could have lost a first-rate journalist because he wasn't paid what he deserved. Maybe I should look for a new job.

• BONUS SIN •
Being Selfish

I know bosses come in all sorts of styles. I know everyone has their methods. My view is if you do whatever you do well, it works. You can be a tough boss, a soft boss, an absentee boss; it doesn't matter. Just execute. But one thing I can't abide is bosses who put themselves first and their employees second. And by that I mean focusing on their own careers and not the careers of the people under them.

My original model—the good boss kind—was former *Boston Globe* sports editor Don Skwar. In my *Boston Globe* days, back in the eighties, Don ran the hottest sports section in the country with the top writers in the business. His folks wrote books, appeared on TV, and were the go-to writers if you really wanted to know what was going on in the sports they covered. Don seemed to be very quiet. I wondered what it was like to run the most powerful sports section in the country yet have such a low profile. He wasn't famous, so what was the point? I figured it out. It was because his job was to make sure Jackie MacMullan (who helped write the awesome 2009

Larry Bird/Magic Johnson book *When the Game Was Ours*) was the star. And columnists Bob Ryan and Dan Shaughnessy. Not him.

Don helped me out with a decision years later, as it turns out. The Gerald Loeb awards, which are designed to honor business journalists, have a prize for editors who work behind the scenes. (A rule that has been violated in spirit over the years, but that's too inside baseball to even bring up. Even though I just did.) Writers know them. Their bosses and their writers know them. But outside of the industry, no one knows them or even cares. At the time, a couple of people were planning on nominating me. That would have been nice. But I had someone on my staff who was, in real life, perfect for the award. He was an editor who regularly saved troubled stories and made great stories better. He was our unsung hero at *Fortune.* Would I have loved to win that award? Sure. Did I think about just nominating our guy a year or two later? Sure, for a second. But I remembered Don Skwar. We nominated a terrific, godlike story editor named Tim Smith and he won the award. It meant much more to him than it would ever mean to me. (Well, I'm lying a little.) But no big deal. That was my job.

You're Fired!

☛ For those of you who have never read the Harry Potter books, there's a professor at the witches' and wizards' boarding school, Hogwarts, called Severus Snape. In the earlier books, he taught a class called "Potions," in which students like Harry Potter learned to make concoctions that would allow them to do battle with evildoing storm trooper types, like the Death Eaters, by disguising themselves as someone else. The classroom was creepy, the professor was creepier, and there was a cloud of fear that always hung over the place. Harry and just about every other student hated Snape. He's a pretty unlikable guy.

That's how I always feel when I have to fire someone—like I'm Severus Snape. I inflict misery and, in return, become an object of fear and scorn.

And no one else much likes that part of the job either. In fact, they actively avoid it. One of the best editors at *Fortune* said a while back, "That's got to be the worst part of the job, firing someone."

"Not a whole lot of fun," I replied. "You ever do it?"

"Oh, no, never," she said. She didn't look happy. (As if I was going to ask her to fire someone.)

"Well, maybe you should," I said in a "this might be a good rite of passage thing" sort of way.

"No, that's okay," she said, shaking her head really hard. "*You can do that!*"

Oh, Christ, I thought later. *I am scary like Snape.*

One thing I learned about being a boss, though, is that firing is an unavoidable part of the job—if you're doing your job right, that is. As obnoxious as it sounds—and trust me, it *is* obnoxious—it allows you to get rid of people who aren't pulling their weight and, at the same time, build a first-rate team. And, believe it or not, it can make the rest of your staff much happier. There's usually a lot of resentment toward workers who aren't doing their fair share. The laggards are often underworked because editors avoid them and talented employees don't cotton to doing more work than second-rate colleagues—especially if those underachievers are overpaid. Those people can also undermine you. We had a couple of mediocre reporter types on my staff who would complain about not appearing in *Fortune*. You'd explain that their story ideas weren't, uh, good. No matter, they would then complain to others on the staff about the big, bad managers (that would be me, for the most part) who were holding them back. You can't have that.

Firing is not only one of the most important parts of any management job, but it's even more important these days, given the pressure many industries are under to cut costs. No one who works for any media company, I can tell you, doesn't think about being fired a couple of times a week because: 1. Their newspaper or magazine is going out of business, slowly and painfully; 2. They are either too old or too expensive (my elderly coworkers once joked that our employer is "No *com-*

pany for old men"); 3. They don't get "new media" and the waterskiing squirrel concept. Or all of the above.

The trouble is that—like my pal—no one wants to fire people. And when they do, they go about it the wrong way. I figured this out pretty quickly at *The Boston Globe* a few decades back. I had just become assistant business editor and, against my will, was assigned to overhaul a story by one of our senior writers, who had a reputation as a sloppy journalist and all-around jerk. As I feared, it took me a few days to get the story into publishable shape. The reporting was mediocre and the writer couldn't string two sentences together that made any sense. I had to do a lot of guessing. He must have been drunk, I thought, when he wrote the first draft. In any event, you had to be drunk to get through it. (Or edit it.)

After this and a little prodding from me, my boss decided he had to go. But instead of calling the guy in and saying, "Hey, you're not cutting it, you're out," he went the indirect route. He offered the writer an assignment he knew he would not take—in a city he wouldn't move to—in the hopes he'd soon quit. He did.

Why the elaborate game of chicken? In this case, my boss was cleaning up after someone else, so why go through the heartbreak of confrontation? This writer was allowed to produce substandard work for years—probably because his previous bosses were impressed by some important people the writer called friends. And you don't want to fire someone who knows important people! (This happens more than you think. I once supervised a writer who some famous CEOs liked a lot, partly because he would never write negative stories about them. Pretty soon, he started thinking he was as important as they were. I swear that's the only reason he survived. Some people are born with talent; some people are born with the talent of becoming pals with people who have talent. I hope you all follow that.)

But what you have to really understand about many bosses is that we're basically, as I've said, cowards and bullies. It's just the way it is. If we don't like your work, we will rarely say it straight out. Confrontation isn't a whole lot of fun and it's not on any list of reasons why you sign up for a tour of duty in management. So you come up with a whole bunch of elaborate games to avoid telling people what just needs to be said. My wife, Catherine, once handed me a quote from someone who said the best way to fire someone is to get them so mad at you that they'll quit. I don't know if that quote is all that well known, but the practice is.

Newsweek—which may or may not be out of business by the time you're reading this—was a festering breeding ground of such behavior back in the nineties. I never met, during my five years as a senior editor there, a more dysfunctional, albeit talented, group of managers. Why be honest with someone when it's so much easier—and a lot more fun—to stab them in the back and watch them slowly suffer until they give up and quit?

I know because I was a victim. Almost. The editor of *Newsweek* at the time didn't think much of me right off the bat. Why? We had different views of what my section should cover. I believed we should run stories no one else had. His investment banking pals whispered in his ear that we should follow *The Wall Street Journal* headlines. As in: "You guys ought to tell readers what was in the headlines last week just in case they missed it." Whatever. The point is that the editor wanted to fire my ass. But, of course, he would never tell me this directly. He would, instead, send an emissary.

✖

The messenger was another manager, who, by the way, was always very good to me and was one of the smartest guys on earth. So I don't want you to get the wrong idea. But still . . . when I was about to go on vacation, he walked into my office. I thought he was going to say good-bye, have a good time, and bring me back a T-shirt or something. But instead he told me the big guy wasn't cheery about my leadership of the business section and, during my two-week break, I ought to take the opportunity to think about "how you can do things differently." Or, in other words, "work on your résumé." (Note to readers: DO NOT EVER do this to an employee, no matter how awful he is, before a vacation with his family. Or force someone else to do it. Not even if you hate him. You WILL burn in hell!)

Of course, both my boss and his boss would have saved themselves a lot of time if they just said, "Hey, we're not pleased and maybe you ought to look for another job." Nah, too easy. I wouldn't suffer. About a month or so later, I had lunch with the guy who wanted to fire me, at a "fine" restaurant, of course, and confronted him. "I understand you aren't happy with my work. Look, if you aren't, just tell me and I'll leave." Unbelievably, he said everything was okay. "I'm very direct," he said. "If I have a problem, I'll let you know." Yeah, right. Okay. Fine with me. I guess I still had a job. As it turned out, he ended up liking me just fine, largely because I hired a lot of good people and produced stories that readers talked about. But the culture at *Newsweek*, in the old days anyway, was to let problems drag on and on until somebody else had to deal with them.

The moral to this story is that your job as a manager will be a whole lot easier if you tell your employees what the hell you're actually thinking. If you're doing the job right, you're helping people be better and, if they're not cutting it, you help them improve or fire them. And the way you go about it says a lot about you and your company and how your stars feel about working for you. The folks who still have jobs have to trust that you're not harboring deep and ugly feelings about them, that you're not, in secret, Professor Snape.

I promised in the introduction that I wouldn't torture you with Six Sigma or anything along those lines. But anyone writing these kinds of books can't really resist, and I do have a few good rules to help you through this most unpleasant of tasks. Here they are. I can't guarantee they will work for you, but they sure work for me. Most of the time.

Fire Fast

Sounds cruel, huh? Well, just between us, it isn't cruel at all. It's a good thing. In fact, you're a cold-hearted troll if you don't take care of business quickly. I also call this "the rule of respecting other people's lives." Let's go right back to *Newsweek*, the death star of management. There was a young man I'll call "Barry the Reporter." Barry had been toiling at the magazine for years hoping to become a writer, moving up from the ranks of eager fact-checker. Well, Barry the Reporter was a great researcher. But he wasn't all that good as a writer—and had a snowball's chance in hell of ever becoming one at *Newsweek*. "Don't give that story to Barry, he can't write" is something my bosses would often say. Or, "Don't even think about giving him a raise or a promotion—he's never going to get better." Too bad his bosses didn't let him know. By the time he woke up a decade later he was well into his thirties with some of the best work years of his life behind him. He could have been working on Wall Street, getting rich, and soaking thousands of Americans. Or maybe he could have been helping people at a nonprofit somewhere. Anything. So what would have been more humane? Firing him early on or letting him languish for years in a job he had no chance of excelling at? You make the call. And you know what? No one cared that they wasted a decade of Barry's working life.

I never forgot Barry. Later, when I took over *Fortune Small Business*, I was having trouble finding the right people. Although, as I've said, the magazine was a great place to work, it was relatively unknown and thus didn't attract top-shelf talent. The staff was a mix of young and old, semitalented folks. Some were literally exiled from *Money* magazine, a sister publication at Time Inc. that was overseeing the publication at the time. I remember my first meeting with the staff. I walked into the conference room and I immediately recalled the barroom scene in the first Star Wars movie, where, in the dark and dingy Mos Eisley Cantina, a collection of criminal and unsightly aliens bickered, entertained themselves, and conducted business as Luke Skywalker looked on. (I would absolutely rent the movie just to see this. I'm waiting for someone to write a Mos Eisley Cantina app, too.) It was a strange bunch. They were sad and confused. I couldn't blame them. How would you feel if your bosses thought you were subhuman? A number of these folks could have had great careers in other professions. If only someone had told them they weren't cut out for major-league journalism. (By the way, I knew this because the previous editor was kind enough to evaluate each writer. I also saw their work in the magazine; it wasn't pretty.) It took me a few years to work through the staff and send many of them on their way. I hope, in some way, they appreciated that I got them off that dead-end street. But since they didn't know the story of Barry the Reporter, I'm sure they still think I'm an evil son of a bitch.

Don't Play the Body Language Game

A few years back, I was sitting in the office of my brand-new boss. I was left over from the previous administration.She had been a hotshot editor: ultrasmart, clever, and really self-assured. Everything I wasn't, to be sure. She was even cool. (I think she got an offer to run a fashion magazine at one point, but I was afraid to ask her.) I was worried that she wanted to pick her own team and I'd end up in the Mos Eisley Cantina. I told her I didn't want to wake up a year from now without a job and forced to get food stamps. "If you don't want me," I said in so many words, "it's okay. I just need to start looking for another job."

"Gee," she said. "I thought things were going well. Wasn't my body language good?" Body language? What's that about? Well, if it's bad "body language," apparently the employee will then expect to be fired and actually be relieved when it finally happens. Thus, he or she won't demand a lengthy explanation. That would cut into valuable lunch time at the Four Seasons. (This is not to be confused with the "assign them to another city" method of rejection.)

It's hard to say what "good" or "bad" body language is exactly, but you know it when you see it. Think of a first date (or your spouse) when the person you're with really doesn't want to be within ten feet of you. That's bad body language. You can just tell. Then, think of your boss doing the same thing. The trouble with this is that your employees spend their days looking for signs they're in good favor. So if you come to work one day with a bad back, it could send someone into a weeklong panic. The bad body language method has other variations. In my business, you ignore the unwanted at meetings and dismiss their ideas out of hand. Even good ideas. (Rule number one: no eye contact.) Or don't invite them to certain meetings at all. That's bad body language by omission.

Sometimes you have to avoid people because you're not ready to have certain conversations. But for the most part, just tell them the bad news and get it over with.

Give Them a Head Start

HR folks and corporate lawyers don't like this, so proceed with caution. But if I know I'm going to have to fire someone—and believe it or not, you may know this within a month or two of hiring the person in question—I always like to give people time to find a new job. I had an employee, whom I like too much to name, who was a senior writer and specialized in what we call "soft" stories. She wrote light pieces about funny Super Bowl ads, entrepreneurs with wacky ideas like talking mops; that kind of thing. At the time, at *Newsweek*, we were becoming a bit more hard-core with writers like Allan Sloan and Jane Bryant Quinn, who at times were like vampires sinking their teeth into their victims. Tough writers doing tough stories, in other words.

My bosses thought Miss Softie didn't fit in, even though they had promoted her just a few years earlier. I didn't mind having her on the staff—you do need all types—but I went along with their request to fire her because I wanted to develop a more aggressive team. The conversation with her was painful. She couldn't understand why she was being fired when she had been promoted just a few short years before. (Not by me, by the way. It was one of those "sounded like a good idea at the time" promotions.) I'm not sure I explained it well, but the gist was the makeup of the team had changed. I needed a different kind of writer. However, I came up with a good offer to protect her and her family and manage to avoid a lawsuit. I told her she had a year to find a new job. If she found one in twenty-four hours she'd get her severance payout. If she found a job fifty weeks later she would get the payout. She was happy—or happier, anyway. I was happy I could make life a little easier for her. Her coworkers were pleased because we treated her right. Somehow, the HR department went along with this. I must have gotten them on a good day.

I'm not going to pretend you can do this now. Company lawyers and numbers guys try to prevent such deals. Still, it made sense. I had one employee recently who I swear was going to go out and hire a lawyer after he had been told the bad news. It took two months of extra severance to get him to sign his termination agreement. And I didn't ask anyone to sign off on it—I'd rather not spend days in court. But giving him the extra time eased the panic. And when people panic, they hire lawyers.

Don't Let Anyone Else Do Your Dirty Work

One of the biggest mistakes you can make is to let someone else, like your boss, fire your direct reports. It diminishes you in the eyes of your employees and peers. I've seen this done many times and it is bad. This usually happens at larger companies. A lot of people just like to push the job off on their deputies. That way, they'll always be the good guys. The best bosses always do the firing themselves. They want to show the rest of the staff that they're not afraid to take on unpleasant tasks. You do not want to be perceived as a wimp. In other words: never let anyone do the dirty work when you're running things.

I remember a time a few years ago when a publication was changing editors and undergoing a job purge at the same time. The top bosses decided to spare the new editor the trouble of firing many of the old crew, which he planned to do anyway. Maybe they figured he should come in with a clean slate. But from my point of view, it backfired. Many of the folks who remained—I know, I talked with them—felt like it was a sign of weakness on the part of the new guy. They would have respected him a lot more if he did the job himself. I think it took a few years before the writers who remained got over that and discovered their leader was a straight shooter. I never forgot that.

Give Them a Chance to Resign

I'm not much of a rule guy. But having a little structure helps bring a little dignity to the process and also keeps the union folks off your back. At many places I've worked, we have a probation schedule. It's called "managing" a person "out." Nice, huh? It goes something like this: You first have to have a "conversation of concern," which results in a thirty-day probation. The other stages are "Oral Warning" and "Written Warning." An employee, at the end of the day, gets a ninety-day or so head start. Sometimes more if you're feeling kind.

If you're lucky, it will never get that far. Most people are smart enough to know that a conversation that ends in "If you have any further questions, call Monica in HR" means that unemployment is in the near future. (I have taken people off probation if their performance radically improved. But that's rare. By the time you get to that stage, you usually know there's no hope.)

So if a firing chat goes well, here's what it should sound like: "Steve, this is what we call a conversation of concern. That means we're worried about the quality of your work. For example, your last story on the president of the Poughkeepsie Steel Company was written in what resembled an ancient language. That may cut it at certain publications, but not here. You have thirty days to improve your work. If you don't, we'll give you an oral warning and you'll have another thirty days. If you still don't improve you'll get a final thirty days and be in real danger of losing your job. Any questions? No? Good. If you think of any, feel free to call HR. They'll discuss any options you might have. (Translation: a severance package.) And by the way, I have to be honest. While we'll help you in any way we can, I don't think your chances of success are all that high. I hope I'm going to be surprised." (Translation: You're really fired. Really.)

Now, I know this sounds like a cop-out. That we're not being direct and honest. But your hands are really tied. You can't fire rank-and-file folks in a company like mine without adequate warning. (Well, you can, but it often gets messy.) But you're certainly being straight by doling out the warning in the first place and saying you're not optimistic. Think of it as a ninety-day freebie.

Give Them a Soft Landing

If you're really doing your job right, the person you're letting go should feel as good as she can possibly feel walking out the door. I know this sounds pretty silly. But there are ways to give her a little boost of confidence if you care. At least you won't suck out her soul.

About a decade ago, I hired a very tough and talented young lady and was pretty happy about it. She seemed to have a nice way with words, was a good reporter, and loved doing the hard stories. The tougher the better. My kind of writer.

But, as often happens, she froze up when she started writing magazine pieces. I have no idea why good writers choke. Do they see polished, finished products and assume they'll fail if they can't reach that level in their first draft? When I worked at *The Wall Street Journal*, the idea of appearing on the front page of a national newspaper seemed to spook a lot of writers. It reminds me of when the former New York Yankees second baseman Chuck Knoblauch all of a sudden had trouble throwing the ball to first base. It was a slow, cruel professional death no one could explain.

In any event, it was clear that, after a few months, this young woman was never going to get the ball to first base. I called her into my office just before her probation period was up and fired her. She was frantic. What was really odd was that she was more concerned about being fired than about losing the job. "I've never been fired," she said. "Why are you doing this?" "Look," I said, "this has nothing to do with talent. You have that. If you got a job at a newspaper and someone told me a year later you won the Pulitzer, I wouldn't be surprised. You just weren't cut out for this magazine. There are too many people on the staff with your precise skills. I need a shortstop, not a second baseman." (And certainly not Chuck Knoblauch.)

I know, I know. Sounds kind of dumb. But it worked. She understood that she was talented but she didn't fit in our plans. Nothing wrong with that. ("It's not you—it's us!") I've used the baseball analogy for years. It works and it helps that I also believe it. And I do believe someone can succeed elsewhere if they don't work out for me. The woman I fired, I swear, felt better about herself after leaving the magazine. Better than she felt working at the magazine, that's for sure. Jack Shewmaker, at one time the late Sam Walton's right-hand man at Wal-Mart, once told me he loved searching for store managers from failed retailers—or store managers who just washed out elsewhere. More often than not, it was just a bad marriage. Or their bosses just cast them badly. Made sense to me.

Notes from the Other Side

It's easy for me to sit here and tell you how to fire someone. But I also have perspective from the other side of the fence.

It was a few months before the end of 2009 and everyone at Time Inc. knew that layoffs were coming. (If you didn't know it as an insider, you could read about it in the newspaper and Web sites that covered the media.) In a strange way, it was a relief I wasn't a part of the downsizing process—frankly I was tired of participating in what was becoming, it felt like anyway, an annual ritual. I was tired of avoiding questions from writers when I knew the answers. I was tired of doling out clues to folks who were just hoping I would give them some hint (a wink, a thumbs-up, a high five) that their jobs were safe.

I was basically at peace with whatever was going to happen. I knew, from dealing with *Fortune*'s budget for a number of years, that some high-priced folks would have to go. All I asked of my bosses was that I be told quickly. I started planning it all out. I would finish writing my book and put together a slew of editorial projects. I talked with a friend about starting a business and renting office space on the Hudson River. But then reality set in. During a day off, writing this book, I was struck by how quiet it was at my home office. The phone wasn't ringing. No one was knocking on my office door asking for raises or feedback on a story idea. How many phone calls would I get a day? How many phone calls would I be making looking for work? How many hours could I spend at the gym? The gloom set in. Meanwhile, there was no indication that my bosses would tell me anything soon. So this was what it was like to be left hanging. (They couldn't tell me anything as it turned out, because they didn't know.) I got a number of phone calls from people, including those on the business side of the company, asking, "How are you doing?" That roughly translates to: "We heard you may be on the way out and are wondering if you heard anything yet." Nice!

I was resigned to the fact that my time had come. (Hell, at least it would provide a good ending for the book.) I knew the numbers better than anyone. To reach the goals that were set for the magazine the following year, well-paid vets like me would have to go. As I told a friend, "There aren't enough $50,000-a-year junior reporters to whack." It was, for sure, a nerve-racking time. The good thing was I could be honest with my colleagues. I could tell them to expect anything and "even I might be part of the group to go."

I was convinced I would be gone in a few short weeks. I knew, at the least, that my boss was deciding between me and another editor with roughly the same amount of experience and salary. That editor and I actually talked about it. The bake-off amused us. We had different skills but were equally valuable. Why would a good team even think about doing that? Dwyane Wade or LeBron James? Well, sort of like them. But why would you even make that choice? After the holidays, I finally got the answer: I would be staying. I have to admit I had mixed feelings. I could have taken my severance and finished this book and embarked on some sort of new adventure. Part of me was looking forward to that. I wasn't sure I wanted to stay and go through this all over again. But I did like my boss, a terrific guy. I liked the magazine. I liked my paycheck.

I'm not quite sure why I was the chosen one. I can't honestly tell you what I do that other journalists can't do. I suppose I can do most things well. Others can only do one or two things well. I suspect behind the scenes some of the writers were lobbying on my behalf. Whatever the reason, it was good for someone like me to go through the long weeks of uncertainty. Maybe I can spare someone that misery in the next round.

Never Worry About Being Fired Yourself

This chapter is about not being afraid to fire employees and, more important, about doing it the right way. But I'm going to flip that on its head just a bit. I think the worst thing you can do as a manager is *be afraid of being fired*. It leads to all sorts of bad decisions. You would *never* do some of the things I suggested in this chapter if you worried about getting fired. You just wouldn't. For instance: would you even think of giving anyone extra severance without asking the HR department if you thought your next paycheck would be coming from the state unemployment department?

Getting rid of that fear changed my career. In the late seventies, while I was working at a newspaper in Connecticut, I found myself struggling. I wasn't a very good hard news writer, preferring to come up with my own ideas and writing feature stories. I tried to do what my bosses wanted, but I just couldn't. One day I just didn't care anymore. I told my boss to put me on probation. I think my exact words were: "If you don't like my work in six months, I'll leave. Just let me write the pieces I'm good at, instead of forcing me to write stories I hate and don't do particularly well. You have a whole staff of folks who can do those for you."

He was dumbfounded. An employee putting himself on probation? That was a first. I think he was so surprised that he agreed to my conditions. And I wrote what I wanted to write and the results were pretty good, by twenty-seven-year-old, suburban journalist standards.

I eventually left the paper, a few months later, in fact. I kind of hated everyone I worked for there, so it was okay. But, hell, it actually freed me up.

Now, it took me a while to really get with the "I don't care about being fired" program, I have to confess. I was kind of a mess when I wrote my first front-page story for *The Wall Street Journal* in 1984. (As most *WSJ* rookies are, by the way.) I had just turned in the story draft and hadn't heard anything from my boss, Kathy Christensen. I finally got a phone call and Kathy said, in what I can only describe as an "I'm going to fire you as soon as you get here" voice, to come down to her office right away.

I actually had something resembling an anxiety attack. "Damn," I thought, "I just got my dream job, and now I'm going to be fired, and I'll have to call up my old editor at the trade magazine and beg for my old job back and find a new apartment because I'm paying too much for the one I have now; and I'll have to tell my friends, who won't be my friends anymore because I don't have an important job—and what am I going to tell my mother, who is so proud that I got this job in the first place? And what am I going to tell my old boss at my former newspaper who was going to fire me and I then called him to brag about being hired by *The Wall Street Journal*? I'll be humiliated!"

I thought all that and more, to tell you the truth. (It was like the dream sequences in the movie *Inception*, which seemed to go on for days, but were only a few minutes in reality.) I had to prepare myself. I finally got to Kathy's office, in all of thirty seconds. And, damn. She wasn't alone. Sitting with her was Norm Pearlstine, the editor of the paper. For sure, I was getting fired.

"Sit down," Kathy said. Now I was really sure. "Hank just wrote one of the best (front-page) stories ever for a new hire." I looked at Norm and he said, "Great, let's get it in the paper." I don't think I said anything. Maybe a feeble "thanks." I got up, walked quickly to my desk and called my mom. And just about vowed never to worry about being fired again. It was more stressful than actually being fired. (In case you're wondering, I've never been fired from a journalism job, even though now that I've written this sentence I probably will be. I've been fired from jobs as a waiter. One time, for example, I refused to bring dinner to my two bosses in their office in the restaurant's basement. I'll leave the reason they asked me to do this to your imagination, but I was soon out of there.)

A number of years later I was talking withone of my peers. She was a bit amazed that I said "no" so often to the business managers of the publication—about things like advertisers requesting certain story topics. But I explained to her that's the way I viewed my job. "Right or wrong," I said, "I say what I think." And that, I can say, started with my anxiety attack at *The Wall Street Journal.*

Not that I haven't been worried since. Once, at *Newsweek,* one of the writers was concerned that top management was blocking stories about a certain company and a big advertiser. We took our boss to a coffee shop and complained about it. We also pointed out that this little problem was never leaked to the press. The message: if you continue to obstruct our stories, that's what would happen. It wasn't the greatest career move on my part. In fact, I think that was the end of any chance of promotion at *Newsweek.* (More on this coffee shop episode later.) But I had to do that for my writer—and for me, frankly. A lot of folks worried about job security would have avoided that confrontation altogether.

Optics, or Paying Attention to How Things Look

☛ January 23, 2010: I was sitting in a coffee shop in Peekskill, New York. We were near the end, it seemed, of the worst financial mess anyone of my generation has seen. At the least, it felt like we were on a break from it. People, who weren't investment bankers or anyone else flying on the fumes of Wall Street, were seething about bailing out an industry full of trolls who act like they aren't to blame for anything that happened. I had just read a piece in *The New York Times Magazine* about the executives of AIG, saved by the U.S. taxpayer, whining about restrictions on their year-end bonuses. Cash up front, they said, was necessary, because some of them had "second and third homes and alimony payments." (Can you believe anyone would say this to a journalist? It was just another example of how incredibly clueless they were.) Meanwhile, on the front page of the newspaper, in the same issue as the magazine piece, was a heartbreaking story about a woman who was thankful for the food stamp program. I can guarantee you she wasn't worried about coming up with the mortgage payment for her "third" home—or supporting her ex.

Is it just me or is there something wrong about all this? If you talk privately to Wall Streeters, they don't understand why us common folk can't understand their point of view.

They're suffering, too! But they are paying, in one way or another, for it. If you think about it, it's a great lesson in management. In other words: how you act—and how people react to how you act—matters.

In boss land, how you behave and how things look is more important than almost everything else. What do your decisions look like to your employees and to outsiders? How do you act in a crisis? How do you react to an employee who isn't doing his best work? How do you deal with other executives at your company who are treating your employees unfairly? Do you defend them? Or do you do what most people do—blame them and make your own boss or investors happy?

It all starts with transparency, which, when you think about it, is what this book is all about. You have to be honest with your employees, you have to be honest with the outside world. At least most of the time. People think that PR is spin, but good PR is honesty, which was really lacking during the financial crisis, and subsequently the BP oil spill and Johnson & Johnson's botched recall on some of its children's medications. I can't help but think of Ricky Gervais's character in the movie *The Invention of Lying*. There's a great scene when he's on a first date with Jennifer Garner. She's on the phone with her mom talking about Gervais's character, the schlumpy screenwriter, Mark Bellison. Garner's character, Anna, says he's kind of an UGH and there's no way he'll ever get a kiss out of the evening, never mind anything else. And she's saying this on her cell phone right in front of him while they're out to dinner. Cruel, sure. But at least poor Mark knows where he stands and can save some money on dessert and the tip. There's something about telling the truth, right away, that's lost on a lot of us.

Now, as I admit throughout these pages, I'm a lot like everyone else when it comes to being completely open. A few years back, we had layoffs, as we did for many of the previous years. Did we learn anything after years of creating unhappy employees? Not really. We knew there were going to be layoffs, but we insisted on not openly talking about it because our HR folks insisted on our not openly talking about it. I wasn't all that silent. When people asked if there were going to be layoffs, I would say: "I can't tell you but it ain't going to be cheery. I could go. You could go. Who knows?" I think people got the picture. (I was surprised that even though I hit folks in the head with clues, some were still shocked when the axe eventually fell.)

Everyone can agree that layoffs aren't a good thing. What's worse than layoffs? Holiday layoffs. So what did we do? We laid off a bunch of people right before the holidays and were left with a staff that wasn't particularly cheery or loyal. And I couldn't blame them. There was no reason to trust me or any of the senior management. I'm sure writers we've tried to hire have thought twice about joining us as a result. Simply put, we forgot that our actions are perceived by others, not just ourselves. We forgot about the rules of optics.

Advice from the Coffee Guy

Howard Schultz, the chief executive officer of Starbucks, is one of the few executives that I'm actually jealous of. He gets to be around good coffee all the time. He created one of the country's great businesses. He's fifty-two years old but looks like he's thirty-two. He's got a lot of hair. I'll stop now. But the one other thing I truly admire about Schultz is that he knows the value of treating employees well. He also understands how fragile employee loyalty is if you do the wrong thing and lose their trust. It's hard enough to gain in the first place, but once you've lost it, getting it back is really tough.

Starbucks, as most fans of business know, is well known for providing health care benefits to both full- and part-time employees. That's pretty cool. Because if you know anything about retail, you also know that it isn't a paternalistic business. It's kind of like those war movies about ancient Greece and Rome when thousands are sent into battle, killed in grisly ways and then replaced by thousands more. If you die, that's okay. There are more who will fit right in. That's retail. So why spend money on health insurance? Your workers will come and go and you just replace them. (I am, of course, exaggerating a bit. But not much.) Well, Schultz knows there's a good business reason for this. Better benefits means more qualified and more loyal employees. Loyal employees mean less turnover, which means you reduce your training costs and customer service is a lot better. The lines move faster. (Starbucks' turnover, by the way, has been historically among the lowest in retail.)

Now, it's not all that difficult to be a good, do-the-right-thing kind of guy when things are going great. When you're a growing company riding the wave, being generous doesn't cost you much. It's good pub; you get on covers of magazines like *Fortune*; you get rich; you're a genius! When things go sour, though, it's hard to fight the impulse to be a little evil in order to get ahead.

Starbucks once had one of those bad runs a few years

ago—specifically, 2007–2009. Schultz had stepped aside, but his replacement overexpanded and then the economy tanked. Schultz eventually stepped back in and took over day-to-day control of the company. His job, among other things, was to get Starbucks through the pain of restructuring while maintaining the culture it had taken him decades to build. He did a number of tough things, such as closing stores and shedding a lot of jobs, which didn't endear him to his legions.

But he wouldn't mess with the one thing the company was famous for: providing health benefits to employees who worked at least twenty hours a week. His moment of truth came during a discussion with one of the company's big shareholders. He, the shareholder, suggested that the tough economy and the company's other problems were a perfect excuse for cutting back on the generous benefits. But Schultz wasn't keen on the shareholder's request. He understood how bad it would look.

Here's how Schultz recalled the conversation. "We had an investor conference in December of 2009," he said. "That was the low point when the stock was seven or eight dollars a share. In the thirty days leading up to that [conference] we were receiving lots of different phone calls based on what people thought we should do," like franchising the mostly company-owned stores. One day, Schultz received a call from a big investor he had known for a long time who told him, in effect, that the company had to slash costs. "Howard, I feel very strongly that the company has to make very serious decisions and cuts. . . . The cost of health care is one thing you can no longer afford . . . this is the time to cut health care benefits. You've got all the cover in the world. Everyone will understand you had no choice."

Schultz responded, "I wouldn't do that under almost any circumstance." Cutting those benefits, he added, would destroy "the level of trust with our people." The investor wasn't finished and cut Schultz off. "You're missing the point," the investor said, requesting that his call be shared with the board. "This is what you need to do to survive."

"Listen," Schultz said, "with all due respect. If we did anything like that we would no longer have a company... we'd lose the trust and confidence of our employees. We have to maintain it and preserve it . . . we can't kill it while we navigate through this crisis." Schultz felt so strongly about this that he told the investor that, if he disagreed with his decision, he could choose to sell his shares in the company. Schultz also refused to discuss the call with his board. Cutting medical benefits wasn't happening. Period.

Schultz understood the rules of optics in other ways as well. During the big wave of layoffs, he delivered the news of the cuts himself, via a webcast, to every employee in the company. On the surface, it doesn't sound like a big deal. But it is. I've been at places where the boss announces cuts by e-mail. Schultz apologized for the cuts, took the blame, and explained why the company had to close so many stores. He then did something that mattered a lot to the employees who were left behind: about 70 percent of the people who lost retail jobs were placed in outlets within just a few miles of the stores where they originally worked. He also made sure the process was fair. For instance, when it came to management jobs, "I went through every name myself to ensure that there was no politicking or maneuvering. I wanted to see specific justification for why someone was on that list." In other words: no friends taking care of friends. That kind of stuff makes a difference and the message gets around.

If you don't think this kind of thing matters to employees, let me tell you the story of Kmart versus Wal-Mart. Now, it kind of seems silly today that at one point these two retailers were even in the same ballpark. (Today, Wal-Mart is, by sales, the largest company in the world—and Kmart? Basically an afterthought.) But they were fierce competitors back in the day. And Kmart was powerful enough, at one time, to entice celeb homemaker Martha Stewart to lend her name to a line of home goods products.

I covered the two companies for a trade magazine and later for *The Wall Street Journal* in the eighties. At the time, Wal-Mart was well known in the business world and to those of us who wrote about retailing. But I could never understand why Kmart was so weak and Wal-Mart was so strong, until I visited a Kmart store to see one of the new Martha Stewart home goods departments. Now, Kmart must have spent millions designing and installing these new departments. But as I walked in, I saw boxes all over the floor—some empty, some full. It looked like someone had started stocking shelves and promptly took a twenty-four-hour lunch break. So all that thought, money, and planning was thrown out the window because a couple of minimum wage workers just didn't care that much. Meanwhile, you could walk into basically any Wal-Mart and the shelves were well stocked, the stores were clean, and you could actually find someone to help you. Kmart was another story. I swear, if you wanted to carry out a cash register, no one would stop you. No one seemed to be around.

Wal-Mart, meanwhile, seemed to figure out that retail

success lies in the hands of your lowest-paid employees. So they gave employees stock options and money back if they cut down on theft and generally made them feel like they were as important as their bosses. There was a little smoke and mirrors about all this—later they forgot the things that made them great and got into trouble as a result. (More on Wal-Mart to come.) But at the time, management did care enough to make their employees feel like they were important to the company's success. Kmart didn't, and they have been on the ropes for years.

Many CEOs are pretty blind when it comes to optics. For example, in the nineties, I was involved in a cover story for *Newsweek* written by Allan Sloan, which I edited and helped conceive. The concept was simple: The economy was doing okay—by the numbers, that is—but people in general were feeling terrible. Why? Because corporate America, "sucking up to Wall Street," as Allan put it, was cutting tens of thousands of workers in what seemed to be a gratuitous and arbitrary way. We felt, as we wrote the outline in a Hard Rock Café in Manhattan, that we had solved the puzzle. That we had figured out what executives were doing wrong. It wasn't about economics. It was about optics.

You could argue that you cut 10 percent of the jobs to save the other 90 percent of the workforce. (This must be in a PR manual somewhere.) We never bought that theory, but why get involved in the debate? It was partly about the way things looked. That's what these companies didn't understand. They certainly didn't understand that if people are worried about their jobs, they don't spend a lot at the mall. It was a point lost on businesses and their PR armies.

The poster boy for all this was Robert Allen, the CEO of

AT&T. His story should be a must-read for every executive and MBA student in the country. Talk about a cautionary tale. Allan Sloan interviewed Allen about all his layoffs and what seemed like his heavy-handed approach to them. Robert Allen, whose mind must have been occupied by stock-analyst aliens at the time, said something like "What do you want me to do? Go on TV and cry?" Sloan called back the AT&T PR man and, as a courtesy, ran the quote by him. Yup, Allen said it. He didn't seem to care. That put the AT&T chief in the bad PR hall of fame.

Bob Allen had no idea how this looked to the outside world, and he fired a lot of people trying to make Wall Street happy, ruined lives, and then had the balls to say, "Hey, that's life. Tough noogies." We called it "In Your Face Capitalism." One of my favorite writers, ESPN's Bill Simmons, might call it "Eff-U Capitalism." Whatever it is, it didn't look good. I'm happy about one thing: because of our story, I think PR advisers everywhere now make their bosses at least *seem* like they care when they have to kill off workers. Maybe they've even sweetened severance benefits as a result, though I wouldn't actually be surprised if they didn't.

Wall Street, as I said, has been going through the same thing. Although ordinary folks are struggling, Wall Streeters have held on to the notion that they deserve their hefty bonuses. But the brain-dead reasoning produced some unintended consequences. Now, they may indeed deserve the bonuses. For one thing, it's part of a regular pay package. The word "bonus" is kind of misleading. They work crazy hours—far more than I do. They also live in places like New York where the cost of living is very high. Now, no one really cares all that much when the economy is humming along. But when it isn't, that's when Main Street blames Wall Street for everything. It doesn't matter if Main Street is right or wrong, that's the way many people feel. There's this old saying: "It doesn't matter if you're cheating on your wife. It matters if she *thinks you are.*" Wall Street never understood that and to this day doesn't get it. You can see it in their response to any PR. Always a step behind the news.

For instance, when Goldman Sachs announced a plan to help small businesses in 2009 by providing half a billion dollars in grants, no one cared because the gesture didn't seem genuine. Other companies increased stock payments instead of cash payments. (As if stock isn't real money. We aren't that dumb—are we?) They point out how much money they give to charity. But they never, unless before the cameras in Congress, seem to say they're sorry. One can almost imagine these bank executives agreeing to be waterboarded before agreeing to show any empathy.

The consequences? New rules—some good, many not—and federal agencies launching investigations around the clock. Wall Street asked for it and got it. Now, this may seem to have nothing at all to do with you and how you relate to your employees, but it absolutely does. If you do bad things to your workers, you'll have consequences. If you are faking it, people will see right through you and act accordingly. Here are a few rules to live by.

THE DON'T LIE RULE

I've broken this one more than I care to admit. ("Uh, nice job on that Jones Industries profile. I just have a couple hundred things I'd like you to change.") But I do believe it. I don't think

I've ever made a writer happy when I've killed their story—and explained why. But it looks a whole lot better to them and others, later, if you're honest about it. For one thing, when the compliment comes, it actually means something to them because they know you're telling the truth.

BE KIND TO ALL EMPLOYEES, EVEN IF THEY DON'T DESERVE IT

The way you treat one employee sends a message. Now, I've never met a manager who has shed a tear for those who are actively incompetent. That's largely because these same employees are also the most troublesome. They complain more and also tend to agitate others. (That's one of the great mysteries of management: why do the least talented folks complain the most? Because they're frustrated about not being any good? Or they're looking for someone to blame for their lack of success? Probably both.) And they usually rile up your more talented workers. If you don't handle it right, you can alienate your stars.

While I was at *Newsweek*, one of our top writers was unusually sensitive to the problems of others. When someone was fired or treated poorly it had an impact on her and some of the other stars. She was truly angry when a colleague was mistreated, even if on the surface he may have deserved it. I figured it was a matter of time before she, loyalty to *Newsweek* aside, would look somewhere else for work—and she eventually did.

THE TOYOTA RULE

As I sat down to write this chapter, Toyota was still grappling with the scandal over the sudden acceleration of some of its cars and other quality woes. The problem with the cars is disturbing, of course, but it's a fascinating case for management types. It isn't clear how many Toyotas had this problem, but it probably is a very small percentage of its cars. The company really took a hit by *appearing* to be shifty. By refusing to confront the problem directly and recall cars immediately, Toyota lost trust with its customers and regulators. Let's face it, 2010 wasn't a good year for big business.

After Toyota came BP and the worst oil spill in U.S. history. Like Toyota, BP tried to figure out who else to blame. No one bought it. Chevron figured it out, though. An oil pipe broke in Utah. When it happened, I was listening to a radio report. The story ended with "Chevron takes full responsibility" for the accident. Tell me, after these two incidents, which company you would prefer to buy your gasoline from, let alone work for?

THE PAGE SIX RULE

For any student of optics, this rule is the ultimate litmus test for personal conduct. Page Six is the gossip page in the *New York Post,* which everyone in the media world reads religiously. (It can also appear on page four or five, which I don't understand. I guess it's just the *Post,* where accuracy is something for other news organizations to worry about.) At *Newsweek,* we always had this expression when discussing any sort of controversial issue: "How would you feel about it if that appeared on Page Six?"

Let me give you an example. Let's say my publisher came to me and said Ford would pay me half a million dollars if I said something nasty about Toyota. And let's suppose I took the money. How would it look if that appeared in the press? Really bad. That's the Page Six Rule. You can also call it The Facebook Rule. My kids would call this Old Jerk Rule, but I don't care. There are a lot of people doing really stupid things on Facebook. A friend of my son's, a really smart Ivy League kid, once posted a photo on her Facebook page of herself clearly bombed on something/everything at a party. How does that look to the law school admission folks at Harvard? Or an employer?

Imagine what your decisions would look like to others.

THE SANDY WEILL TONE DEAFNESS RULE

I'm always amazed at what stupid things really smart executives say. Sometimes, after running our morning meeting at *Fortune,* I walk into my office and wonder why the hell I told a certain joke or commented, inappropriately, on a writer's story. I guess we can call this the Sandy Weill, or Lloyd Blankfein, or even the Hank Gilman Rule, because we all do or say things that don't sound or look good to others. Sandy Weill, the former Citigroup chief, once came to *Fortune* to talk about his education initiatives. He really does a lot of good work in this area. But it annoys me to no end how executives constantly blame teachers for any failing in the system. It's not the parents, it's not the resources, it's not the test-crazy system that forces educators to teach from a fill-in-the-oval guide. It's always the union-loving, lazy teachers who have tenure and summers off.

Okay, fair enough. Let's say all that is true, which it isn't, by the way. I asked Sandy, what if we raised teachers' salaries and you attracted "more talented" people to the profession? And rewarded the best teachers already in the system? Oh no, he responded in so many words, "we find that money has nothing to do with quality." I see, I said. "So money is a reasonable incentive for your Wall Street folks, but not the rest of us?" It was one of the dumbest things I have ever heard a smart man say. He had no idea how that would sound to others. In that case, me.

Lloyd Blankfein, the CEO of Goldman Sachs, had a similar problem with optics, but the stakes were a hell of a lot higher. During the height of the financial crisis, he was interviewed in England and joked about how Wall Street in general, and Goldman in particular, "was doing God's work." Well, some folks might have found that funny. But anyone unemployed or worried about losing their job was in no mood for Blankfein, he of the megamillion-dollar bonuses, to brush off complaints about his company with a joke. He had no idea, it appears, what that would sound like. It also showed, or appeared to show, how Wall Streeters really felt about the public outrage over their role in triggering the recession. "Hey, they'll get over it. It's all a game. We really are more important than anyone else."

THE PROZAC RULE OF UNINTENDED CONSEQUENCES

Finally, sometimes you mean well and it just doesn't work out. It's not your fault. It's often just bad luck that you stumbled into a burning building. You really mean to say or do something that shows you're an understanding boss and your employees totally come away with another message.

Back in my early days of management, I thought that being a bit playful with my staff was a good thing. You know, if they think you're a fun-loving knucklehead every once in a while it will help when you really have to come down hard. I always kept a basketball on my desk. One day I called out "Catch!" to one of our reporters across the room. I threw a perfect two-handed pass. Unfortunately, she didn't look up and then, smack, the ball hit her in the face. Instead of the fun-loving knucklehead, I'm the idiot, jackass boss. (Who was lucky not to get fired.) I didn't think of that unintended consequence.

Nor, recently, did one of my Time Inc. bosses. She didn't throw a basketball, but the result was the same. At a lunch with people from around the company, she said she was worried everyone was stressed out and working too hard. (So far, so good . . .) That they should put away their BlackBerrys when they got home and actually have a life for once. But then, to prove her point, she mentioned that she was stunned by the number of Time Inc. people who were taking antidepressants. (Not so good . . .)

Now, her heart was in the right place. Her message was that she was concerned that her employees were working their way to ruin. But a lot of folks read it this way: "Oh my God, the boss is checking up on our prescription drugs. She *has* that information. And uses it!" Now, there was no way she meant it that way. But in a company filled with people who are worried about their jobs, you could see why paying attention to your words is so crucial.

So why is this all so important? Why fret about "how

things look" when your bosses are happy with you? After all, paying attention to optics is hard work. It's always easier to say or do things and not worry about how people feel. You can always find new employees, right? You can always find another job. But that approach never ends well. A former star in my business spent a good part of his career not caring about such things. He was rude to people. He verbally abused his employees. He broke all my rules of optics and kind of got away with it because he was so talented. (Or was blackmailing his bosses.) But when it finally came time for him to look for a job, everyone in the business avoided him. They'd heard all the stories. He's now "consulting."

You can't hit folks with basketballs forever.

Yes, There Is Something You Can Learn from Wal-Mart

One of the best case studies of a company that finally "got" the rules of optics has to be Wal-Mart. It doesn't seem so long ago that the retailer was viewed as the most evil company on the planet. There were stories about Wal-Mart locking workers in stores overnight, ignoring overtime rules, discriminating against female employees when it came to pay and promotions. (Us worry? That kind of stuff is for wimpy Hillary Clinton fans to fret about.)

The company hasn't gone all warm and fuzzy on us. (As I write this, it would like to take a class action suit against it by former and current female employees all the way to the Supreme Court.) But Wal-Mart's execs seem to have gotten the image thing down.

It, of course, helped that Wall Street became the devil. And the poor economy is always an ally of Wal-Mart. But the company did a lot of smart things nonetheless, particularly its former chief executive Lee Scott. For one thing, public relations is no longer viewed as a cost center. In the old days, they didn't even have PR folks, as far as I could tell. (And if they did, they hid them in old nuclear bomb fallout shelters.) Now, they cooperate with reporters—even if they don't like it—and manage to get some good news about the company out there. Scott came up with more healthcare coverage for his workers, became a spokesperson of sorts for the uninsured, and emerged as an evangelist for the green movement, if you can believe that one. (As much of an evangelist as you can be working for a company that paves over grass fields to build 100,000-square-foot stores. But those small bottles of All detergent are pretty cool, I must admit.) Scott and the company were also a lot quicker to admit mistakes, like the time Wal-Mart tried to recover insurance settlement money from a worker who suffered brain damage in a car accident. It's just not easy running a company with more than 2 million employees. Someone is bound to screw up.

But just making fewer mistakes— and recognizing that what consumers think of you matters—goes a long way in repairing the damage.

The Well-Behaved Manager

☛ **My favorite fictional boss** is Bill Henrickson of the HBO series *Big Love.* He can juggle a bunch of wives, a crazy family on a polygamist compound, run for political office, and still manage to operate a successful home improvement store. Like anyone else, he messes up. Or his family does. Like the time he told "wife #2", Nicki (bad mistake), that he suspects one of his office staff outed the Henricksons as polygamists. Now, if you know the character of Nicki, you know that she'll do just about anything to protect the family. So, in a panic, she gets someone to try to run over the employee with a Hummer in the parking lot of the main office. As much as I'm a fan of Nicki, Bill, and Hummers, that was a little rash. But Bill, except for the multiple wives thing, generally has his head screwed on straight.

Like my hero Bill, managers have no idea how to behave in every situation. Sure, you know that you can't do things like sexually harass your employees or run them over with a Hummer. No one, I hope, has to tell you that. A lot of the things good managers do aren't really a mystery; some of these things I already ranted about—feedback, honesty, raises, and making your stars feel at home—are all good. But for me, there are a lot of things that are just ignored by most of us. I'm not saying all of this will work for you. If you're a boss who likes to keep your bosses happy, this is difficult. But, in general, there are a few things well-behaved managers do, and do consistently.

Defend Your Staff

Management is a lot about conflicts. If you don't have the stomach for that, go back to the assembly line. If you're supervising employees, you're telling them what they're doing wrong and how to improve, and you're approving and rejecting their ideas. You're also, at times, in conflict with your peers and bosses. You argue about strategy, personnel, and, in better times, where to have your next offsite. (Bora-Bora was once at the center of an "off-site meeting" debate in the good old days at my place.)

But probably the toughest thing a manager has to do is stick up for his or her employees—largely because there's not a lot of upside in terms of your own career advancement. And it also involves a lot of unpleasant confrontation. And a lot of it goes on behind the scenes, so your employees never see the kind of work you're doing on their behalf. As I mentioned earlier, an editor who worked for me was laid off a couple of years ago and pretty much hates me now. What he doesn't know—because I never told him—was that I was involved in saving his job on at least two other occasions during other purges. The last time, I just ran out of chips to play and he was gone. Sorry.

Now, that didn't do me a whole lot of good with him or the rest of the staff. You just can't pick and choose the situations. If you don't stick up for your folks—make it a habit, in other words—you end up just making your bosses happy. It's got to be your policy. You need to believe it's important.

A few years back, one of the publications I worked for had a top editor whom the staff didn't like and couldn't figure out. She was nice to me, but icy cold, and came off as rude to others. She would actually take a longer route to the restroom—lined with tall file cabinets—to avoid eye contact with people on the staff. Our writers and editors also felt micromanaged at every turn. A number of the staff talked to me about it. The easy way out would have been to let her boss know and he would take care of the problem. But I didn't see it that way. I had to confront her myself. First of all, she would never trust me again. I'd be just another guy who did an end-run and whined to the big boss. But more important, this was my job. I was supposed to help people who worked for me.

The meeting wasn't cheery. I brought along another editor and he ended up just sitting like a lump with a terrified look on his face. So it was up to me. I told our boss that she "was losing the staff" and explained all the problems from the micromanaging to the employee-avoidance techniques on her restroom runs. It was the toughest thing I ever had to do, but the results were good, at least for a while. Her behavior improved, and the staff knew that I'd come to their rescue—and could be trusted to do it again.

Those kinds of situations are rare. Most of the time you're dealing with helping just one employee as opposed to your complete staff. In the previous chapter, on optics, I told you the story of "Corporate Killers," a piece on how companies were playing up to Wall Street by laying off employees. What I didn't tell you was of the conflict with the magazine's editors after the story appeared. There were a couple of things going on. First, the executives featured in the piece, and on the cover, were big advertisers. To the editors' credit, specifically the late Maynard Parker, who liked a good fight, they allowed us—writer Allan Sloan and me—to run with the story.

But I don't think the top editors anticipated the reaction. No one, especially a chief executive, likes his picture shaped into a mug shot and placed on a cover of a national magazine. It's one of those rules of life. (Confession: I knew exactly how they'd react. I didn't tell anyone because I loved the cover.) To placate one CEO, Robert Allen of AT&T, the editors allowed him to write a "My Turn" column, which was normally reserved for everyday readers. (You know, stuff like: "Why baseball means so much to me.") We were livid. Not only was AT&T's Allen given ample chance to respond to the story, but our editors didn't bother to tell us about the column. Basically, they didn't want to explain it because, how do you justify doing a big favor for a well-connected CEO? The answer is you don't. How could you give this guy such a forum when he already had his chance to respond? Would the normal Joe get such a break? No, of course not.

The second part of this tale was that Allan and I wanted to run follow-up stories on AT&T's layoffs. But we were getting the clear signal that *Newsweek* had had its fill. ("Uh, Hank, we're tired of those AT&T stories. Why don't you run something on the new line of Barbie dolls." It was really like that.) Once again we decided to throw a fit. We met with our boss, Parker, in a coffee shop in the lobby of the *Newsweek* building.

He said he wasn't killing our stories. (Somebody else was!) We said, good. But we made it clear we were going to play hardball if we were blocked from covering a legitimate story about the company. Hardball meant talking to media reporters about an advertiser getting special treatment. But we never did because, frankly, no one would have cared. We weren't on that much Ecstasy. (Did it exist then?) Still, I think that was about the end of my career at *Newsweek*. You don't threaten your boss and get a promotion or stay employed long. (I left.) But I also earned the respect of Allan and the staff. For however long I worked at *Newsweek*, they'd do just about anything for me. Well, I liked to think they would. They would probably, at least, lend me money.

Don't Blame Others, and Don't Take Too Much Credit

Okay, you do have to blame others—sometimes. And you do have to take credit—sometimes. Otherwise, you'll never get a raise. But I'm talking about extremes. There are a lot of managers who take a curtain call every time someone under them comes up with a good idea. And, boy, are they fast to point fingers when something goes wrong.

Back to *Newsweek*. A number of years ago a picture appeared on the cover of the magazine of a woman who had septuplets. Heartwarming. Even more heartwarming was that the magazine fixed her bad teeth. (How bad? Keith Richards teeth, if you old-timers out there know what I mean.) Someone fixed them in the photo department or production and *Newsweek* took a hit in J-schools everywhere.

But the sad thing, for me, wasn't that *Newsweek* fixed the woman's teeth on the cover—I thought that was nice of them, actually. (Hell, magazines seem to fix everything on anybody.) The real crime was that some poor sap in production was blamed for it. No one else stood up. And let me tell you, no one in production would do anything like that—fix teeth or make Oprah skinnier—without an editor telling them to do it. The whole thing was just squirrelly.

The fact is, in most cases, you should share the blame or take it all. It's just weak, otherwise. I'm pretty good at it, for the most part. Let me tell you a story. You ever hear of the movie *The Informant!*? It's pretty good. Funny. Dark. Starred Matt Damon. See it. It's about a real-life whistle-blower named Mark Whitacre. He was a high-level exec at Archer Daniels Midland and he exposed price-fixing at the company. Some executives went to jail, including Whitacre, who also committed some crimes along the way and was increasingly unreliable and erratic. *Fortune* put the spotlight on the scandal when it happened in the mid-nineties. When I came aboard, I was assigned to the writer who was working on the story. In this particular piece, the writer quoted from an FBI document that happened to be forged by Whitacre. (That was nice of him.)

How'd we find out about what happened? Well, *The New York Times* wrote a small article about it, that's how. What a disaster. The writer was devastated. But I wasn't going to leave him hanging. I took the blame along with him. I was his editor. Sure, he vouched for the document. But, I figured, I had let him down. I usually ask writers to make sure the documents in their possession are genuine. A simple damn question. I didn't in this case, for some reason. I offered to resign, an offer that wasn't accepted. I'm glad I kept my job. I was happier I shared the shame with my writer. I'm glad I deflected a little of the blame from him because he was a good guy working under tremendous pressure. We, the editors, let him down.

Sometimes I don't know what's worse: avoiding the blame or taking credit for other people's work. At one of the publications I worked for, I came up with a project that eventually became an annual technology magazine. I had the idea and executed it. So I was really surprised when one of my bosses took credit for the creation of the magazine in his professional bio. I never did say anything to him about it. I was more amused than anything else. He *didn't* have anything better than *that* to put on his résumé? Yikes! As it turned out, one of the lower-level reporters involved with a couple of stories also took credit for the magazine's creation on *his* résumé. (He eventually went on to some pretty big jobs. Maybe he was onto something. Can't wait to read his book.) Trust me, readers, it wasn't that good a magazine.

So how do you know when to take credit and when to graciously give the spotlight to someone else? There is a right way to do it. My boss at *Fortune*, Andy Serwer, goes to the other extreme. He gives me credit for ideas I swear I never came up with. But that's the way he is. It's kind of embarrassing sometimes, but a nice gesture. For editors like Andy, it's just a way of doing business. One of our freelancers, David Kaplan, wrote a great piece on Sal Khan, a genius who places video teaching seminars on YouTube. Khan had many fans, including Bill

Gates. The story was terrific. Well written and surprising. "Great idea, David, how'd you come up with it?" I asked. David told me his editor, Leigh Gallagher, heard about Khan at a party and passed the tip on to him. I later went to Leigh and asked her why she didn't take credit for the story. I think she turned her back on me. Now, that's a boss. Leigh came up with a nice idea, gave it to her writer, and then let him have his time in the spotlight.

Do Not Force Your Employees to Abandon Their Families

One of the world's most honest employers had to be Dave Thomas, the founder of Wendy's, who died in 2002. In his obituary, Thomas is quoted as saying that he didn't spend much time with his family because they couldn't stand to spend much time under the same roof with each other. They would, basically, kill each other if they did. Pretty strange if you consider that Thomas named the company after his daughter, Wendy. But then again, it's pretty strange that a guy with a bad heart would spend most of his life eating hamburgers.

Most bosses aren't as honest as Thomas, so I have to give him points for that. You ever read those business profiles where the executive brags about all the hours he works? And the writers have this "Oh wow, you're so big, strong, and great" attitude about it all? A few years ago, *Fortune*'s Geoff Colvin poked a few holes in that act in a profile of GE chief executive

Jeff Immelt. Colvin tallied up the hours Immelt said he worked and found it was impossible for any man to live, sleep, and raise his family based on these calculations. I'm not saying this about Immelt—who does work hard—but anyone who works that long is probably inefficient, killing time in other ways or ignoring his family—or all three. It really all depends on what you consider work time to be. I've seen executives go on golf outings, then thump their chest and tell you how tough it is to put in those fifteen-hour workdays. Yeah, it gets pretty tense when those cart girls keep offering you beer as you're trying to line up a putt. Now, I'm not saying they don't spend a lot of time away from home, but it isn't hard labor.

I really don't care if business folks, or people in my business, want to brag about how many hours they work. But I do care when it affects the people working under them. When workers feel like they have to ignore their husbands and wives and miss their kids' after-school events because the boss has those expectations—or sets those expectations through example—that's a big problem. I got this from someone I work with the other day: "I have to pick up my kids at 5:30 but I'll be putting in two hours of work tonight so don't worry." I said: "No, you really don't need to do that. You work plenty. Spend time with your family." I don't think she listened, but I tried. Here are a few of my rules:

1. CLOCK PUNCHING IS SILLY. I don't care when you come in; I don't care when you leave. I don't care how many hours you work. I care about getting the job done. If the job isn't done and done correctly we have a problem. If it is, go to the beach on Tuesday afternoon if you want to.

2. LIFE ISN'T EASY. Don't beat yourself into a wasted hulk. If you have a demanding job and are raising a family, you can't consistently blow off your spouse and kids and still be effective at work. You will be tired. You will produce sloppy work. You will make mistakes. You will be unhappy. I promise you that. We recently had an editor who let a major mistake slip through a story. He *never* does this. He was tired; we gave him too much work. It was our fault.

3. FAMILY IS IMPORTANT. Send this message through your own actions. I try not to miss my kids' sporting or musical events even if it means walking out of work at 3 p.m. I make sure my work is done. I make sure I'm available. I get in early and take care of what I need to take care of. (God bless BlackBerrys.) I also insist that others do the same with their families or friends. A fellow manager was telling me the other day that he wanted to see his daughter's softball games. I said, sure, see them all. Work on the train if it makes you feel better. Now here was a guy who is working in the office and home all the time. What is he worried about? Must have had a lot of bosses who have no lives.

4. BEWARE THE BOSS WHO IS WORKING ALL THE TIME. It's usually a bunch of bull, to tell you the truth. I knew a guy, who specialized in making his people miserable, who stayed at work well after hours. And God help anyone on his staff who wanted to leave at a normal time. They *knew* not to do that. They lived in fear and watched the clock. Meanwhile, why was he staying? Partly because he was waiting around to meet up with a girlfriend after work. Why get on the train and see your family when there's stuff to do?

✖

5. DO NOT BUG THE OLD GUYS. This one is for the young managers out there—and some older managers who don't know any better. I'm going to share a little secret with you: older workers can't work as many hours at their peak as they used to. Startling revelation, huh? Well, some people don't understand this. They don't like the fact that their fifty-plus employees can't run those twelve-to-fifteen-hour workday marathons anymore, at least without a good sleep sometime during the day. Now, I'm not saying this is always a good thing. Some older workers are just checked out because, frankly, they're bored or just don't care and are coasting until someone catches on. But in many cases, older workers, at least in my business, are a lot more efficient than they were earlier in their careers. They can write good copy faster, execute ideas faster, and know how to report stories more efficiently. In other words: they can do in five hours what their younger colleagues take ten hours to do. Or more.

As for me, I think I'm a lot more efficient than I was when I was a young reporter. Not that I can remember anymore.

Know When It's Time for a Change

It's really hard to explain what Boston Celtics coach Doc Rivers and Sex Pistols singer Johnny "Rotten" Lydon are doing together in a book like this, but bear with me a bit and it will be clear. (This will only happen in my book.) They both serve to illustrate a point I want to make about change. And when to change is one of the great lost arts of management, as far as I'm concerned. When, as a manager, do you step aside? When have you overstayed your welcome? When do you know it's time to move on?

Let's start with Doc Rivers. In 2010, the Celtics made the NBA Finals. But earlier in the year, there was talk that the players were tuning out their coach. They weren't like that in 2008, when they were winning the championship and buying into Rivers's team-first concept. Maybe his philosophy was no longer fresh. Rivers delayed his decision to return. Jump now and spend time with your family or get pushed later? Even though the team was close to winning the championship again, it was aging. If his management style was starting to wear thin last year, what about the next season? Rivers eventually decided to stay, but the point is that all great coaches and managers hit a wall. They become less effective in the same place, with the same group of people, in the same department. It's the classic dilemma. The trouble is that few managers know when to jump and their bosses don't know when to push them.

In my business, the boss usually has six years or so in the top spot. The theory? I don't know why anyone settled on six years, but each leader brings something different for a different time or era. Some are aggressive news junkies. Some are more feature oriented. Neither style is right or wrong. But after a number of years the best editors get stale and don't execute as well and their employees begin to ignore them. They need a new message.

Another sure sign that you should change is showing up for work bored, angry, or both. Let's take angry first. You could resent your boss for not moving on. You could be angry with the company for cutting benefits. (Or merging with a company like AOL, which I and many others were angry about.) You could be tired of your coworkers or upset someone got a promotion you thought you deserved.

At *Newsweek,* I was passed over for an assistant managing editor's job, which would have been a promotion. All of the senior editors, in fact, were passed over. A good friend told me that if you start to arrive at work angry, it's time to go. So I started looking for a new job while my peers remained angry, for the most part. Nirvana's late singer Kurt Cobain used to whine about fame. Someone pointed this out to John Lydon, who responded, "You don't have to be famous, you can just quit." Yup, you can just quit. It's how I feel about some of my colleagues who are upset about their jobs. You *don't* have to work at Time Inc., you can quit. You're not an effective leader when you're always pissed off. You lose focus and people don't want to deal with you.

Boredom is a completely different issue. It's a battle. You can only do the same thing for so long. I asked Howard Schultz why he once stepped aside and let someone else run Starbucks. He said he was bored. In my world, boredom is a bad disease for beat reporters. At *The Wall Street Journal,* we used to always rotate beats. Why? After a number of years on the job, the beat writers would fall victim to the "that story has already been done" syndrome. I had one writer tell me he wouldn't profile a company's founding family because he did it some twenty years or so earlier. So what if a new generation of readers wants to know? Tell them to go to the library.

So am I saying put yourself out of work? Why? Well, it doesn't quite have to be that way, depending on the company you work for. There are jobs outside your company—well, you would hope, anyway—and there are often other jobs in your place. Bill Conaty spent fourteen years at General Electric as the company's top human resources executive and an adviser to CEOs Jack Welch and Jeff Immelt. At GE, he says, the bosses who created strong succession plans were "generally rewarded with bigger roles... which eliminates the fear factor of thinking I'm putting myself out of work." What you don't want to do, he says, is develop a successor and then let him or her twist in the wind. "It was always interesting to watch leaders who dissed their own succession plans saying things like 'she's very good but at least one job away from replacing me,'" says Conaty. That, he adds, "caused us to . . . think we might need to make a change sooner than we thought."

In other words, move over, pal.

Avoid Favoritism (or the Appearance of Favoritism!)

Yup, we're all guilty of this one. Let's face it, you spend more time with the folks on your staff who are the top producers. You have to keep them happy. If it's between having lunch with a star and the writer who can't find his way into the magazine, you have lunch with the star. Every time. But you do have to make sure you spend time with everyone, sometimes.

Back in the late eighties, at *The Wall Street Journal*, I'd sit in a row of cubicles at our offices in the World Financial Center. Every so often one of the executive editors would visit with the troops. One day, one of these execs came down to see what we were up to and chat. And he came down again a week later. And that was the pattern. He also had another pattern: every time he came for a visit, it seemed, he only talked to the female reporters. Never talked to me, though I think he brushed against my cubicle once. Maybe it was because I wasn't a woman. Maybe it was because I wasn't important enough. But the point is it bugged me—after all, I remember this more than two decades later!

I try to avoid this, I really do. I asked one of our employees about it, and much to my horror, all of us editors were guilty. We all had our favorites. And everyone noticed. My friend had drinks one night with a number of young staffers. She was telling folks that she enjoyed her editors and appreciated how much time they spent with her. "Well," said one of the other reporters, "they do spend time with you if you're one of their favorites." My friend kind of backed off after that—she was a favorite. But it was a point well-taken. And a wake-up call, for me anyway. I'm still not great at it, even though I always have my office door open. But there's hope for you.

Don't Ignore the Middle Class

As much as you would probably like to, you can't have a staff completely filled with stars. For one thing, no one will give you the money to do it. I once told one of our business managers that my purpose on earth was to spend my employer's money. I wanted an unlimited budget and I wanted to exceed it. I don't think he found it funny, largely because he knew I was serious. And I was. I wanted to be the New York Yankees.

But even if you had an unlimited budget, you wouldn't want to have an all-star staff. There are too many small and mid-level tasks you need other people to do. Your stars don't want to wash windows and *you* don't want your stars to wash windows either. Why would you pay them to do that? It's like forcing the CEO to run the forklift. (Though, I have to admit, these days all of us have to run the forklift every once in a while.)

But the truth is the nonstars also do certain things that the stars can't. In the magazine business, we often use researchers and fact-checkers who, over time, become more valuable than the writers themselves. You have to reward them financially and, as with your stars, make sure they're doing interesting work.

For others, you have to identify what they do well, and as I said earlier in the book, let them do it. I told you the story about my time in Connecticut when I put myself on probation because I was so frustrated with my bosses and what kind of work I was doing. I was so frustrated that I was willing to fire myself. If my supervisors had been doing their job, they would have realized that I wasn't the best board of education reporter on the planet. But I was a pretty damn good profile writer.

Why didn't they recognize this? Well, it was a pretty warped way of thinking about the reward system in the newspaper business at the time. Becoming a profile or feature writer was seen as a reward for doing a good job on the overnight police beat. You could be the best feature writer on the planet, but you couldn't get that job because you were an absolutely pathetic cops reporter. So you had great police reporters who became bad feature writers and bad police reporters who could have been great profile writers but instead were, well, shown the door. This didn't make sense, but that's how it worked.

It comes down to this. You have to take your nonstars and figure out what they do best. You then make sure they feel wanted and have good career opportunities ahead of them. If they're not good at the police beat, well, don't make them do it. You might actually, to your great surprise, develop a star you never thought you had. Not that I became a star in Connecticut.

Be a Good Micromanager

I hate to admit it, but I'm of a couple of minds about micromanaging. I know most people will tell you that micromanaging is just awful, but I have a different philosophy. I believe there are two kinds of micromanager: the bad kind and the good kind. You'll have to figure out which one you are.

Let me tackle the good kind first. I'm a big believer in hiring the right people and letting them do their jobs. I don't think I'm lazy, which some micromanagers (the "bad" ones) might accuse me of being. But if you hire the first-rate talent, work out the details at the beginning of a project—and give them enough feedback along the way—it can be a good formula.

There's a downside, as you might imagine. One editor I worked with, for example, was absolutely in love with the cheekiness of the London-based magazine *The Economist.* The editors of the weekly often take a random picture, for example, and place it on a story with a funny caption that somehow ties the picture to the story. It is funny, mostly. In a British sort of way. Sometimes I feel like I'm watching a Monty Python movie when I'm reading it (though not as good). Well, this editor, perhaps in tribute, decided that a story on management could sure use a picture of topless native African women to illustrate it. It was stupid and offensive, and somehow his bosses missed it because they were giving the editor a lot of rope. Too much, as it turned out. He was soon fired, which was a good thing.

But there is a good side to this approach. You can develop some pretty creative people if you just let them do their jobs. I worked at some pretty micromanaged places over the years, but sometimes, if you broke out, even the micromanagers could be surprised. At *Newsweek*, which had a pretty rigorous editing system, I produced a magazine as a special project. Aside from my showing him a story list (he had to see something), my boss didn't focus on the magazine until the very end. Even then, he just glanced at the final product. After we published, my boss noted how smooth the process was with fewer controls and wondered if "there was a lesson" for the rest of the magazine. Yup—just let people do their jobs.

Then there's the bad side of micromanaging: when you don't let people do their jobs. My friend Sam Hill, a consultant, a former executive on Madison Avenue (he's not quite a Mad Man but close enough) and a management writer, contends that even the good micromanagers can wreck any organization. "Over time," Hill says, "micromanagers just destroy the people under them." I'm going to give him the last word, because, frankly, I can't say it any better.

"I'm working with a CEO, not a bad guy. But when someone sends him a ten-page presentation, he'll send it back with twelve pages of notes. This is good and bad. It's good in that he uncovers some very useful things. His questions can be probing. The bad news is that when he's done, he's trained his guys *not to get it right.* [My emphasis.] Why? No matter what they do, he'll pick it apart. He's like a three-year-old asking, why?"

Hill continues: "It's a terrific thing if it's on the front end and it's selective and it leaves the responsibility with the owner of the product. On one level, it's attention to detail. But it turns into doing someone else's job for him. So, at some point his employees might say, 'I do bad work for him because I know it doesn't matter.'"

And you know what? They're right, it doesn't.

Managing in a Crisis

☛ **Let's face it.** Most of the time you spend in management is pretty much the same on a day-to-day basis. It's the plot from the movie *Groundhog Day* as played out in real life. But a couple of times a year, if that, you get to earn your keep.

I can't recall, for the most part, all the plays quarterback Tom Brady made during Super Bowl XXXVI when the New England Patriots upset the St. Louis Rams. I do remember the last drive of the game. There were only eighty-one seconds to go. John Madden, the CBS analyst, insisted that the Patriots were too far back in their own part of the field to mount a game-winning drive. Brady, he said, should take a knee, run out the clock, and head into overtime to fight another day. Instead, Brady coolly directed the Patriots' offense down the field and put Adam Vinatieri in position to kick the game-winning field goal. That's what he'll be remembered for. The Patriots, leading for a good part of the game, were losing their grip. Brady stepped up and saved the team, and the game.

I can't claim I was very "clutch" during my early days of management. (I'm not exactly sure I am now, for that matter.) Still, I sure observed the way others dealt with tough situations. What does this have to do with managing people? Everything, really. If you don't handle a big problem correctly, you can end up with a pretty dispirited group of employees. I recently talked to an editor on our staff about a round of layoffs a few years ago. She said I looked grim and unusually serious during most of the process—and that worried a lot of our staff. I can't believe I did that. No one was asking me to play the role of happy-all-the-time SpongeBob. But on the other hand, I shouldn't have looked like the evil Plankton when people were concerned about their jobs. Not a confidence builder.

Damage Control

Somehow, during my career, I've seen a few of the media industry's blowups close-up. The first was in 1984. I had just been hired by *The Wall Street Journal* in New York. I may or may not have gotten my first paycheck. But just when I started work, the Foster Winans scandal broke in our newsroom and quickly became a national story. For those of you who don't remember—or weren't yet born—Foster Winans was a relatively low-paid reporter who produced the then-powerful "Heard on the Street" column. It was a must-read for investors. The column would often break good and bad news about a company (earnings will be soft in the current quarter, market share is starting to slip; that kind of thing). And it, pardon the cliché, moved markets.

Given the second-by-second news cycle now, it's hard to fathom how powerful the *Journal* and "Heard on the Street" were in those days. As a beat reporter, I would attend securities analyst presentations. During one meeting I ran to the telephone (yup, no cell phones) and called in a story (yup, on a pay phone) about Melville Corp.'s somewhat negative earnings forecast. By the time I got to the office, the company's stock had plunged on my report. I had just wiped out God knows how much in market value. Someone, because of me, lost real money. That was weird and humbling.

So you had to be damn well sure you were accurate. And honest. Most of us felt that way. That sense of responsibility was almost a religion in the *Journal* newsroom. The trouble with Foster Winans was he was telling his friends and others what was going to appear in his columns. And they would invest based on that information. For the rest of us, that kind of behavior was like a cross to a vampire. The SEC announced an investigation and all hell broke loose. That was *never* supposed to happen at the *Journal*. What really struck me, though, was how collectively calm the place was after the scandal broke. Norm Pearlstine, the editor, made quick decisions to fire Winans, cooperate with the SEC, and cover the story the way we would cover any other scandal of that nature. The newspaper came out every day and people put their heads down and did their job. There were, of course, complaints about the coverage. Foster Winans was gay and the newspaper, fairly or not, reported this within the context of the story. (The *Journal* told the story of Winans's companion, for example, and the struggle to pay his medical bills.) There was also grumbling about how little the *Journal* paid its writers. If Winans was paid more, would he have been tempted to cheat? Even by *Journal* standards, he seemed to be underpaid. At least some of us thought so.

But Norm got out ahead of the crisis, internally and externally, and I'm convinced that's what kept the flap under control. "My feeling was," Pearlstine said, looking back recently, "you couldn't control the story but you had to get out in front of it. . . . I didn't want to be in a defensive position and look like we were trying to bury the story."

At Time Inc., I got to see Norm in action again in 2004. This time, it was his decision to turn the notes of a *Time* magazine reporter over to federal prosecutors that made news. Prosecutors had been trying to identify the source of the leaks that revealed the identity of CIA operative Valerie Plame Wilson. (Plame's husband, Joseph Wilson, had written a *New York Times* op-ed piece taking the Bush administration to task over false claims that Iraq's Saddam Hussein was attempting to buy uranium. The leak was seen as revenge for that column.)

I can't say that the ride was as smooth as the Winans flap. It wasn't. There was bitterness about the decision that was so close to the hearts of journalists. Simply put: could you no longer protect your sources? (Pearlstine's parsing of language regarding "anonymous" versus "confidential" sources didn't play well.) And a lot of us were suspicious that our corporate parents at Time Warner were in no mood for a fight. But it could have been a lot worse. Norm calmly explained his reasoning. You may not have agreed with it, but it was clear, and thoughtful. Pearlstine, a lawyer by training, spent hours studying case law—Watergate, the Pentagon Papers—before making his decision. There were "contentious" meetings with *Time* magazine's Washington bureau. But as with the Winans case, Pearlstine kept ahead of the story. "I don't think anyone said you haven't thought about it," Pearlstine recalled. And it wasn't likely that "anyone who disagreed" with the decision "had done as much work as I did."

This isn't to say there wasn't any damage internally; that certain employees didn't feel betrayed. But the damage was contained because Pearlstine took a course of action, stuck to it, and was available to explain himself.

My Time Inc. colleagues may not agree with me about Pearlstine's performance. But then again, many of them never saw how badly management can bungle a crisis.

In contrast to the Winans and *Time* cases, the 1996 story of "Anonymous" at *Newsweek* was mishandled and resulted in a few years of bitterness and tainted a few careers. Background: Joe Klein was a star columnist at *Newsweek* and a terrific journalist whom I know to this day. He decided he wanted to tell the real story of the Clinton campaign through a novel based on his reporting. I don't know, journalistically, how this quite works. Usually, you're supposed to get real people to say real things and write stories about that. Most of us wouldn't take this approach, but so be it. In any event, Joe did the right thing at the beginning: he went to his boss, Maynard Parker, and asked him for permission. Maynard granted it and also was sworn to secrecy. The book, which was titled *Primary Colors,* was published in 1996 under the byline "Anonymous." It became a big hit and garnered national attention as political journalists tried to find out the identity of the author.

There are, right off the bat, a couple of things wrong with this. For one thing, how can you write fictional accounts about the people you cover? No one would have cared if the book wasn't a success—but the search for "Anonymous" became a sport in the press. And this is where it all unraveled. A few reporters asked directly if Joe was Anonymous. He and *Newsweek* said no. So they fibbed.

But *Newsweek* also decided to participate in the "guess the author" game. Jonathan Alter, *Newsweek*'s fine columnist, speculated on a couple of people who didn't happen to be Joe. (He was one of those journalists who asked Klein if he was indeed the secret author.) The editor of the magazine knew Jon's speculation was just flat-out wrong. Still, they allowed it in the magazine. They deceived the people working for *Newsweek*, and they hurt Alter by allowing him to print false information. And at the end of the day, they lied to the readers and advertisers: our customers. Once Joe was outed by *New York* magazine—a professor at Vassar College cleverly produced a computer analysis of the book and connected the writing style to Klein—*Newsweek* went into the scrambling mode—it was like they were calling audibles every time they approached the line of scrimmage—and screwed up about everything they could screw up. And the staff was left demoralized. Let's count the ways.

"WE DIDN'T DO ANYTHING WRONG"

Probably the biggest mistake *Newsweek* made was trying to justify the decision to let Joe do the book and then cover up for him. The staff was furious, and all the excuse making made it all the worse. I remember sitting at a meeting with Maynard Parker asking him if it was now okay for my business writers to write fictional accounts of the people they covered. He said yes, but you knew he didn't mean it. That would be the day. But writing fiction about people you covered wasn't the only sin that was justified; it was lying about it once you were caught.

If, for a minute, you agree it was okay for Joe to write this book under a phony moniker, you have to also agree that *Newsweek* could have had its cake and eaten it all, too. So could Joe. "Okay, you got me. I'm the guy," he could have said, once he was identified by *New York* magazine. The book would still be a best seller and the talk show appearances would have been off the charts and *Newsweek* could have maintained its dignity. But they decided not to.

GOING AGAINST OUR STANDARDS

Letting false information into your publication is a cardinal rule of journalism and completely discredits you. No way, no how, could this ever be excused. I don't even know how you talk yourself into justifying this one. I can only think that the editor was so intoxicated with the idea of this book that he lost all sense of right and wrong. Maynard was once quoted as saying this was more akin to "Who shot J.R.?" as opposed to a national security issue. In other words, what was the fuss all about? But I hadn't known we were in the TV drama business. (But maybe we were.)

SCAPEGOATING

This was a morale killer, as far as I was concerned. Maynard, at one of our morning meetings, told Jonathan Alter that, in essence, *Newsweek* wouldn't have printed false information if he *were a better reporter.* So, follow this. If Alter figured out that Joe was Anonymous we wouldn't have printed false information. It was his fault. Right? I can't follow that reasoning, but that's what it was like in that meeting. One freaking fever dream. Many on the staff, including Alter, were livid. I believed that many, including me, were considering leaving (but wimped out, of course). But the message was this: if something goes wrong at *Newsweek*, we'll find someone to blame and it could be you. No one who worked there ever forgot that.

SCAPEGOATING 2

Well, Joe himself was a victim. He was blamed by management for denying to reporters that he was Anonymous. Yet, at any time, management could have told him to stop. Instead, Joe was forced to write an apology (on Waldorf-Astoria stationery, as if he were being held hostage by a bunch of journalism professors) to the staff. He was also brought in to apologize to the editors.

The only problem was many of us didn't blame Joe. We blamed management. He played by the rules for the most part. By the way: the meeting was apparently leaked by *Newsweek*'s PR staff to *The Washington Post*'s media columnist, who wrote about it the next day. I'm not sure the column ever blamed management, but it portrayed Joe as a man begging his colleagues for forgiveness. My belief: the article was a thinly veiled attempt to convince Washington Post Company editorial executives that Joe was to blame—not the editor of *Newsweek*. I don't know this, but that's my conspiracy theory. At least, it's what some of us thought at the time.

NO ONE WAS HELD ACCOUNTABLE

Really, no one that mattered, except Joe maybe. He eventually went on to write for *The New Yorker* (he's now at *Time*). So he paid the price, although he landed great jobs, and *Newsweek* was the loser because of that. But Parker, the editor of *Newsweek* at the time who died in 1998, kept his job and probably shouldn't have. It sent the wrong signal to the staff: if you're high enough on the totem pole, you can do just about anything and keep your job. Maynard, other than this, in my experience, was an extraordinary editor. A good man. I enjoyed working for him. If there was a hall of fame for journalists, I would have nominated him. But the "Anonymous" dustup was his fault and he blinked in the crisis.

I'm not quite sure what I would have done. But the inability to calmly deal with the "Anonymous" rumpus hurt the magazine for many years—at least internally. I believe to this day that Parker could have solved a lot of this by: 1. Calling it a day when Joe's identity was revealed; 2. Explaining to the staff why he approved the book; 3. Apologizing right away (see Toyota, Wall Street—pick a firm, any firm—and BP for other examples of failures in this area); 4. Taking the blame right away; 5. Making sure false information never got into the magazine. He could have simply told writers he didn't want *Newsweek* in the "Anonymous Hunt" game.

At *Newsweek,* I could see how easily the bond between staff and management could be broken. I'm not sure I learned that lesson entirely until I was at *Fortune.* Anybody following the media business will know that print journalism, or any kind of traditional journalism for that matter, has been in a free fall. It doesn't make for a pleasant work experience. You sit around talking about exit strategies on one hand, and on the other you talk about how you're kind of lucky to be doing this kind of work—and you'll ride the horse for as long as you can.

The real trouble begins when you try to BS yourself and BS your employees. In 2008 and 2009 anyone with half a brain knew that we were struggling. But for some reason, we felt it was important to the staff to go over the financials and show there were signs of hope. So one of the business executives put on an elaborate dog and pony show to prove that the worst was over—and our peers, in fact, weren't doing as well. We were gaining market share! But the PowerPoint just left the wrong message: no, you won't be laid off. Well the layoffs did come in 2008 and they did come in 2009, and now employees worry about it on an annual basis. I'm not here to say that we should be a social service agency. But neither do you pretend things are okay. It's not fair.

Proactive Crisis Management

I'm going to leave the last words on crisis management to our friend Jim Collins. A few years back, Jim and *Fortune*'s Jerry Useem wrote about the best all-time CEOs. Their theory, in the case of Johnson & Johnson's James Burke, was that a CEO often does his best work before a crisis hits a company. In other words: be prepared to do battle. If, for example, it was a rule at *Newsweek* that writers couldn't create fictional accounts of the people they covered, perhaps "Anonymous" would never have happened. Perhaps if Johnson & Johnson itself had followed the words and actions of former chief executive Jim Burke, they wouldn't have gotten in a jam over quality problems in their plants back in 2010.

We'll let Collins explain it. "In business, one of the best examples of effective leadership in crisis that I'm aware of is Jim Burke" of Johnson & Johnson, who is famous for making all the right moves when poison was found in capsules of Tylenol. "But . . . the reasons J&J did so well with the Tylenol crisis related more to what Burke did *before* the crisis emerged, not what happened during the crisis. Here's what we wrote [in *Fortune*]: 'Burke's real defining moment occurred three years before (the Tylenol crisis), when he pulled 20 key executives into a room and thumped his finger on a copy of the J&J credo. Penned 36 years earlier by R. W. Johnson Jr., it laid out the "we hold these truths to be self-evident" of the Johnson & Johnson Company, among them a higher duty to "mothers and all others who use our products." Burke worried that executives had come to view the credo as an artifact—interesting, but hardly relevant to the day-to-day challenges of American capitalism. "I said, 'Here's the credo. If we're not going to live by it, let's tear it off the wall.' (Burke told this to the authors of the book *Leadership and the Quest for Integrity*.) "We either ought to commit to it or get rid of it." The team sat there stunned, wondering if Burke was serious."

He was, and the room erupted into a debate that ended with a recommitment. Burke and his colleagues would conduct similar meetings around the world, restoring the credo as a living document. No one could have predicted the act of terrorism perpetrated on J&J customers in 1982. But J&J's response was predictable. It didn't debate whether customers' safety outweighed short-term financial concerns because the debate was already done. As Collins and Jerry Useem point out, Burke doesn't get credit because he led the company through a crisis; it was because "he led in absence of it."

This is all in striking contrast to Toyota's woes in 2010. The company, stung by complaints about cars with sudden acceleration problems, was paralyzed by internal debate before they eventually did the right thing. They cared too much about the cost of the potential recalls and not enough about their customers. It will go down in business history books as the anti-J&J. (Though J&J ran into a few troubles of its own with over-the-counter medicine recalls in 2010.) Toyota may be right about the cars' problems—that the troubles were isolated—but it doesn't matter. They handled it all wrong because they did not know how to behave. They forgot about the customer. They choked in a crisis.

The Modern Manager

☛ Let me give you a little quiz. You send a long e-mail to your boss about a new project proposal late on a Friday afternoon. This is important to you because you're trying to make the case that one of your coworkers doesn't know what he's talking about and is going to get the company in a whole lot of trouble. You're secretly thinking that your argument, which amounts to about 300 words or so, is so brilliant that it will, no doubt whatsoever, lead to a promotion or a big raise or both. At the least, you'll get a better bottle of wine from your boss during the holidays.

On Monday morning your boss replies "OK."

What the hell does that mean? Well, there are several possibilities:

1. "Okay, I got it. I'll give it some thought and get back to you."
2. "The e-mail is way too long and I'll get back to you in a couple of months."
3. "This is really stupid. You're an idiot. Why are you bothering me?"
4. "This is good stuff. Let me think about it and we'll talk later this morning."

The trouble is it could mean any one of those things—or all four. That's the problem with e-mail. And, like it or not, that's the way we communicate now. It's the primary way for managers to deal with all the things they have to deal with. Mike Duke, the fairly new CEO of Wal-Mart, makes sure—every day—that his in-box is empty. And he has 2 million plus people working for him (not that I'm suggesting that Bob in housewares from the Shallotte, North Carolina, store has his e-mail address). And it's a good thing. I text employees, I e-mail employees, I call employees. But the biggest chance to misinterpret someone is through e-mail. Yet no one gives any thought to how nuanced e-mail can be and how it can really screw everything up if you're not careful. People get all tied up in knots for days trying to figure out your real intentions whenever you send a poorly worded or thought-out e-mail.

I get into endless debates about this and other forms of electronic communication with people. So, in this chapter we're going to go through a lot of things. How you manage through e-mail; what things you should and shouldn't do electronically (Facebook and LinkedIn and so on); and what you should probably not let your folks do—but let them get away with anyway (tweet).

Rules of Electronic Engagement

A couple of years ago, my colleagues at *People* magazine, one of our sister publications at Time Inc., came out with a manifesto on the correct use of e-mail. They called it the "Ten

E-mail Commandments." It was generated by a debate over BlackBerry/iPhone addiction, which some of my management peers believe leads to lower productivity, lack of sleep, and all sorts of other workplace dysfunctions. Well, maybe. I think of it a little bit differently. E-mail, as far as I'm concerned, is one of the great management tools of the last century. You can execute decisions faster, dole out feedback faster, and keep in touch with more of your employees more often. Here are a few things to consider, or rules, if you like, roughly based on the *People* manifesto.

CUT TO THE CHASE

You should do this most of the time. There's nothing more painful than a long e-mail filled with useless information. It's right up there with a Facebook posting on the laundry detergent you've been using. But there's nothing wrong with adding a personal touch, especially when you have to deliver a little bit of bad news. "Hey, your story needs a lot of work. Please call. By the way, did you see the last Knicks game?" Kind of takes the edge off and sends a signal to your employee that your boss still likes you. And friendly is a good thing unless, of course, you have another message you want to send. In that case, keep it short and make them wonder.

AVOID DISCUSSIONS ONLINE

I agree that you never, ever want to discuss personal problems or any kind of information that could have legal implications over e-mail. (As Eliot Spitzer is quoted as saying in my colleague Peter Elkind's book *Rough Justice*: "Never talk when you can nod. And never nod when you can wink. And never write an e-mail because it's death. You're giving prosecutors all the evidence we need.") Tiger Woods would have a thing or two to say about that. But there's nothing wrong with a standard give-and-take that bears no resemblance to sexting. You can't always be on the phone, and e-mail provides a way to make a connection with your employees quickly.

Some people are more comfortable telling you what they really think via e-mail. Mel Tillis, the country singer, has a stutter. He doesn't stutter when he sings. And I'm sure he doesn't stutter when he e-mails. (Not sure he even does, though.) It's the same thing as "meeting pressure." A few of us just can't be ourselves with a room full of colleagues, but we actually have something useful to say. That's why e-mail is a good thing.

DON'T E-MAIL YOUR FOLKS WHEN IT'S EARLY, REALLY EARLY, OR REALLY LATE

Okay, I'm a sinner, largely because I'm up so early. Here's the problem: when you send out e-mails at odd hours, you can send your employees into a frenzy. "Jeez, is he expecting me to wake up at 4 a.m. to respond?" Or . . . "He's up all night working—is that what it takes to be a success at this company?" It can lead to all sorts of psychotic reactions. I know, I've had those episodes. But most of all, I feel sorry for people sending e-mails in the middle of the night. It can mean all sorts of bad things.

DEATH TO "REPLY ALL"

I hate "Reply All" almost as much as the dreaded "CC." You only reply to everyone because you're in mortal fear of keeping anyone out of the loop—and having to explain to them why you did it later. Avoid it unless you really have to keep a bunch of people informed. Except if you're saying something really nasty like "What the hell is John doing on this e-mail trail—he's an idiot." (On second thought, that might be interesting.) "CC," as I said, is another big problem. Some people "CC" the boss on all e-mails because they want to show how smart they really are. I had a bad habit of doing this early in my career and have felt shame ever since. I really hate the "BCCers," because they're just sneaky and can't be trusted.

USE CLEAR SUBJECT LINES AND ONLY ONE SUBJECT LINE PER E-MAIL

My colleagues at *People* really did come up with this one. And I only include it here because it shows how you can overthink this stuff and drive your employees absolutely batty. (Imagine being reprimanded because you didn't get the subject line right!) I don't agree with this, as you can tell. Do you really think people do things like list twenty items in the subject line? Let's see: "Re: The trouble with Sally's latest draft; Tom doesn't like his file cabinet; Bob's ammo stash." I enjoy writing unclear subject lines as well. In fact, I want everyone to waste hours a day thinking about subject lines. (Disclaimer: I am in no way ridiculing my colleagues. I love their list, really.)

RESPOND TO EVERY E-MAIL

This is a big one for me. See the section that follows. You should always respond to e-mails. Not responding—or waiting too long to respond—sends many bad messages, most of which are unintended. (Also see Mike Duke earlier.) It's also not polite. You only refrain from responding when you're the "CC." Then again, I always say "thank you" to telemarketers.

Face It: We're Slaves to E-mail

My biggest pet peeve is "response rate." It may sound like I'm overthinking all this, but if you can't deal with your e-mail, you can't manage people these days. You absolutely can't. If you're a boss you just have to answer all your e-mail and you have to answer it fast. It's a big part of the job. I had a boss who would always put his e-mails aside. He figured he'd answer them, within an hour or so, in a quiet moment. But there was really no telling when he'd get around to it—if at all.

There are a lot of things that can go wrong when you do this. (Does the sender think I'm not important enough? I think that all the time.) The fact is most people, at work that is, send e-mails that are important to some degree, so they deserve a timely answer. You owe it to them to make quick decisions. Let's say you're working on a tight schedule in my business, publishing. Someone wants your blessing on a story idea. If you take too much time to answer, here's what happens: The writer doesn't start reporting until she gets your okay. The photo department doesn't assign the pictures. The art department can't start a layout or even think about it because there's no story yet and no pictures. The production department can't schedule press time.

On any given day there are a couple of dozen e-mails that fall into that category. If you're slow about answering them, you can see how an organization can come to a halt. Should you answer e-mails on vacation and in the evening? You know, whether you like it or not the world has changed. I can't function on vacation if I don't know what's going on at work. In the past, I'd dread getting that phone call from my boss telling me, while I'm on the beach somewhere, that something terrible just happened that I'll need to deal with when I get back. It always happened pre-BlackBerry.

Now, I check in once a day on vacation and feel better that I haven't missed a thing. Let's face it, the day of the out-of-office notice is over. Is it messed up? Sure. But I don't think there's one boss out there who doesn't want to know what's going on at all times. Too much happens; too much can go wrong. My neighbor and his wife made a pact one vacation not to use their BlackBerrys. But my pal got nervous and slipped into a spare bedroom to sneak in a little BlackBerry action. Who was in the bedroom when he walked in? His wife, sneaking in a little BlackBerry time of her own, of course. I'm not endorsing this. Just saying that's the way it is now.

E-mail Disasters

There are a whole lot of things that can go wrong when you're not paying attention to e-mail. In many cases, you end up sending "messages" you never intended to send.

I have a friend I text with a lot. (I know, texting is a different breed of cat. But a lot of the same rules apply.) He always says "yes" or "no" or "ok." Never more than a couple of words when responding. He thinks he saves time that way. I say when someone says "ok" it means they'll go along with whatever you're proposing, but they're not thrilled. What would it take to say "OK, thanks . . . cool" or something like that? Maybe another two seconds. My friend and I wasted a lot of time arguing about that. It happens that way in e-mail, too. I've had, over the years, the occasional employee who uses "okeydokey" as a response, which I hate more than anything. I want to wring their necks. It makes them sound like an idiot, to begin with. (I will never give anyone a raise who says "okeydokey." Never. Message to anyone who works with me: you have been warned.) It also is an insulting response. Here's how I read that one: "All right, I'll do it. But you're a freakin' idiot and I'm only agreeing with this because you're my boss."

Here's another answer I hate: I sent a message to one of my bosses suggesting a new project for our magazine. He sent back a message saying "That's reasonable." Not sure what that meant, but I read it as "Your idea is mediocre." I've known my boss a number of years. I know how he reacts when he likes an idea. He didn't do that this time. I would have preferred he just said "That's a bad idea" and left it at that. "That's reasonable" reads more like "That's reasonable . . . well, not really."

The "hidden message" is bad enough. The absolute, number one sin of e-mail is the "Angry E-mail." I don't know if you have noticed, but e-mail has emboldened some pretty shy people. (For you history buffs, this trend started with "Letters to the Editor" sections in newspapers, then talk radio, and, finally, blogs and tweets.) They get to say things they would never think of saying in person. Then there are those who have never had a problem telling anyone what they think. Both groups have undisciplined trigger fingers.

There's something about anger and e-mail, don't you think? It's as if there's this dark power that forces you to type in the name of the person you're angry with. You ever complain to someone about someone else you're working with? Go slow. At one place—I'm not naming this one, to protect the innocent—one of my former coworkers was being considered for a job in the arts section of the publication. The top editors were debating the pros and cons. You would think they would have such discussions in person. No sense sitting in a room and having a discussion when someone can just jump in and contradict you. Anyway, the author of the e-mail said the prospective arts editor was intellectually challenged and didn't know the Three Tenors from Iggy and the Stooges. (I wouldn't be qualified for this job either.) It was an angry and mean e-mail. Of course, this editor typed in the job candidate's name and pressed the "Send" button. And all hell broke loose.

I don't spend a whole lot of time saying nasty things about my colleagues. A big problem I have is sending responses when I'm angry, tired, or both and I'm particularly susceptible to saying stupid things. In youth sports, they have a pretty good rule that applies to rapid-response e-mail. And that's the "twenty-four-hour rule." If you've ever been a youth sports parent, you know what I'm talking about. Your son or daughter spends most of the game sitting on the bench in the fourth quarter because, well, they're not very good and the coach doesn't want them to screw up the game. You know, deep down inside, this is the right thing to do. But still, your rage builds at the coach who is killing your kid's chance to get a college athletic scholarship. After the game, you walk rapidly toward the sideline and say a bunch of dumb things to the coach and make a total fool out of yourself. The twenty-four-hour rule? If you have an issue with the coach, you have to wait a day to cool down. And usually you do and then tell your child to take up the oboe. E-mail is a little different. The twenty-four-hour rule becomes the twenty-four-minute rule. But the theory is the same.

Social Media

First, full disclosure. You're about to enter this zone with a man in his late fifties. I don't think I'm a dinosaur. I tend to be skeptical, though, and some people interpret this to mean I'm antitechnology. I'm not. I think social media is one of those great inventions that make day-to-day life a lot easier. Like the ATM. Or soft margarine. (Didn't Steve Jobs invent that?) Or, of course, e-mail. To be truthful, I'm afraid to even raise questions about the use of any electronic and/or social media. It must be like the old witch trials in Salem. Say the wrong thing, you're a witch. Even to suggest that something isn't perfect about social networking means you might get burned at that stake. Remember the Internet boom of 2000? If you questioned the business model—where are the profits?—you "just didn't get it." (I think that's when the phrase "the new paradigm" was invented or overused. I'm not entirely sure, but that person should be burned at the stake.)

Anyway, let's get one thing out of the way. I love social media. You know LinkedIn is a great thing, because I can find out what people are really thinking. I was recently asked to "make a professional connection" with a former colleague of mine. I found out she was open to other professional opportunities. Hmm. Considering she had a job, that was pretty interesting. Her boss must have found it interesting, too.

I find it interesting as well. Not that I spend a lot of time doing this, but it is always interesting to find out what your employees are up to. Hey, they don't have to let me in—do they? (Speaking of LinkedIn, if you're looking for a job, is this the place to do it? Don't you want to target the potential employer? Unless someone in Singapore is looking for a software techie, what good is this? Just wondering.)

It gets complicated when your employees start using social media. At *Fortune,* my colleague Jennifer Reingold and I were editing and conceptualizing a story on how employees can "promote their own brand" while, at the same time, toiling for a big company. "Branding," in and of itself, is not a new concept. A number of years ago, *Fast Company* magazine, during its ultratrendy years early last decade, produced a cover with the tagline "The Brand Called You." *Fortune* weighed in with the phrase "You Inc." But these types of stories were basically about people buffing up their brands so they could become successful freelancers or "free agents," as we liked to call them. What's different now is employees at big companies build their own brands via social media. They're not looking to become free agents, but they're getting themselves ready for their next job at another big company. But it's tricky to serve two masters. The story delivered some great examples of how social networking can cut both ways for the company and the "branded employee."

The "Good" was a tale about a Ford Motor Co. executive

who spent a number of years, before he joined Ford, blogging about the intersection of marketing, advertising, and public relations. Ford recruited him. He joined the company, because, he said, he could grow his own reputation while at the same time serving Ford. And he did. He had 3,500 Twitter followers when he arrived at Ford; that figure jumped to 41,000, thanks to Ford. He served himself, and served his master by showing the company how to successfully use social media.

But he had the seal of approval from Ford at the start. What happens if you don't? An employee at a Home Depot outlet in Ohio became enamored with social media, Twitter in particular, and became a self-anointed "voice of the company." He had about 700 followers and decided to organize a town hall meeting so customers could give their feedback. Sounds okay. But he made a couple of mistakes. Number one, he only sent out invitations to his so-called followers. The problem? Well, why shouldn't all customers know about the town hall? And, furthermore, Home Depot wasn't too keen on this inventory control guy in Toledo speaking on the company's behalf. The bottom line: his interests weren't the same as his company's interests, so he was fired. Good branding gone bad.

I can see how social media can help a company like Ford. I can also understand where Home Depot was coming from. All commentators aren't created equal.

We have people who send out tweets on behalf of *Fortune*, mostly to lead folks to interesting stories that we published. Many times they say something smart, but I don't know many people who can consistently say something smart in a few characters. Sometimes they state the obvious. "Boy, were IBM earnings really impressive today." I tried it once. I had nothing, absolutely nothing smart to say. I talked about songs I just heard, news from the music world, because that's my hobby of sorts. ("I can't wait for the new Gaslight Anthem CD!" That's compelling.) I talked myself into thinking that this was all great fun. Two problems. It was a waste of time. The time I spent sending out tweets meant I was spending less time meeting with writers and coming up with story ideas. It's officially sanctioned procrastination as far as I'm concerned. It was also all too public. I did a Google search and there it all was. All the stupid, lame, silly-ass, moronic tweets. All from me. Great career move. (Please do *not* look them up.) I started to panic as well. I felt obligated to say something clever and say it a lot. Too much pressure. I'm blissfully without Twitter now, though my tweets live on in Google.

It's not always a great thing to do your job in public. Let's say I'm a reporter on the computer beat. I'd get to my competitors' Facebook pages, by any means necessary, to see what they're up to. Some talk about what kind of stories they're working on. They talk about their sources. It's one of the great inventions of our time for competitive journalists. I'd also try to find the Facebook pages of key employees of the companies I cover.

So, do you have much of a choice but to tolerate and encourage social networking on the job? You can't ban this stuff, nor would you ever want to. You can't run a business—or cover business like I do—without understanding social media. You absolutely can't. And to understand it, you have to use it. But there have to be some rules. You cannot let your competitors know what you're up to. You can't give your opinions on every event that comes along. Not only is such commentary generally pedestrian, but in my business there are legal reasons and ethical reasons for keeping a lid on it. Could you send out a nasty tweet about the chief executive of Google and ever write fairly about him again? Maybe you think you could be fair, but Google wouldn't know it.

More than anything else, you have to follow my "Page Six Rule" (see chapter 5). And that applies to any form of media. If someone decided to publish what you just said, how would it look?

There's No Such Thing as a Small Role

☛ One thing I've learned throughout my career is that you can get good ideas, and good advice, from, well, anybody. In 2010, I was reading an article in *The New York Times* about the actress Pam Grier, best known for her roles in the 1973 movie *Coffy* and, as I write this, the cable show *The L Word*. In the article, Grier, who, like me, has taken some head-scratching roles in the course of her career, quoted an acting coach who wrote about what I'm describing as the "Small Roles Theory." The theory poses that, whether managing your own career or the career of others, you should never ignore the small roles. You should never blow off the small roles. You should not be hesitant to take the small roles.

If I were to pull aside a young employee and give him or her advice—and I only had one bit of advice to give—this would be it. And that's because one of the biggest mistakes people make during their careers is avoiding jobs or tasks that they feel are beneath them. Or they won't give the same effort when performing small, as opposed to large and complex, tasks. Or they'll wallow in bitterness if they don't get the job they were hoping for. I don't know exactly why this is. It's human nature. Paying attention to this little theory is also great for hiring.

Someone who isn't hesitant about working in the trenches and taking on all sorts of tasks is a good person to bet on.

Back in the early 1980s, I was struggling to find work in between visits to the unemployment office. I finally got a job as a busboy at a deli in Brookline, Massachusetts. The deli is long gone now, and it wasn't the greatest-paying job. I basically lived on tips from customers who appreciated that I kept their water glasses filled. I tried doing the best job I could. I figured if I was going to be a busboy, I might as well be a great busboy. Nothing else to do, really. Every night I spent an extra thirty minutes or so cleaning the food display cases. I inhaled a whole lot of Lysol. When I finally quit, the manager noticed I had indeed become the world's best busboy. He offered me a raise and a chance to be an assistant manager. All because I worked as hard as I could in a small role.

I've used my busboy lesson a lot over the years. The theory breaks down in a number of ways, but first a confession: I can't say I always follow the rule. Like anyone else, I slide. But I can say I follow it most of the time and it has served me well, so I've developed a handy guide to the Small Roles Theory—for both the manager and the employee.

Show Up Ready to Work

You'd be surprised at how many employees and bosses don't do this. A pro basketball player, after a loss, once said that "If I know I gave it my best, I make no apologies to anyone." The biggest struggle I have as an editor is convincing writers to give it their best on the smaller pieces. They often don't because the stakes aren't high. But I judge them on everything, not just their big and meaty projects. At *The Wall Street Journal* I wrote what was called the "Business Briefs" column every once in a while. Normally, you'd see items that small and figure you could make a call or two or copy a press release. But to make them good, you have to call as many folks as you would for a 1,000-word story.

If you don't do that, your work will be just like anyone else's. And if you're sloppy on top of that, you might as well punch your ticket out of town. As a young writer, I was assigned a freelance piece I wasn't keen on for a weekly newspaper in Boston. I don't think I spent much time on the draft and I certainly didn't read the thing before I turned it in. It was a pathetic performance on my part. The editor, who of course had a brain, rejected it and paid me a kill fee—and never talked to me again. To her, the small story was a big deal. And it ended up a big deal for me because I lost a good source of work.

Choosing Jobs

A lot of people avoid jobs and can't see down the road. Those jobs are too small, they reckon. They don't see where they can lead. I have, for some reason, taken a number of those jobs. I can't say I was looking down the road, but I took jobs I thought I would enjoy, even though friends and colleagues thought I was basically crazy. For example, in 1982, I was hired at a magazine called *Chain Store Age*. It's not a place a young journalist aspires to go (though many should). For sure, there aren't a lot of talented people to learn from. But there are some. And the pace and degree of difficulty aren't so challenging. But you learn to push and challenge yourself a bit more.

In 1983, I was heading off to lunch—and for some reason starting to fret that I was a thirtysomething reporter stuck writing about retail displays (called endcaps, if you must know) and the color schemes of discount stores. Not Woodward and Bernstein stuff. (All us young journalists wanted, at the time, to write about things like Watergate and work for *The Washington Post.*) I decided, in that office building on 425 Park Avenue, to write to *The Wall Street Journal* and get the hell out of the trade press. Within a few weeks, I was in for a job interview. An editor at *The Wall Street Journal* saw a couple of things in me. First of all, they needed a retail writer and I seemed to understand business. Always a good thing. Second, I wrote like a *Wall Street Journal* reporter. While at the trade magazine, I broke down the elements that made a good *Wall Street Journal* piece. Once I figured it out, I wrote that way. If I ever wanted to write for the big leagues, my thinking was, I'd better show that I could do it. So even though I was working for a trade magazine publisher, I was still doing work that someone would, eventually, pay attention to. (Kathy Christensen, who hired me, said she recalled thinking that the decision to hire me was "going to be easy.") You always have to think that someone, somewhere, is always watching. I keep on telling my son, the lacrosse goalie, to make sure he works hard on every play of the game. Stay locked in. A college recruiter could have walked in that moment or a high school coach who has a vote in the all-county player tallies. You never know. In my case, I was writing to impress someone and I had no idea who that was. I got the job. If I didn't work for the trade magazine, I might not have ever learned business writing and certainly wouldn't have copied the style of *The Wall Street Journal.*

Sometimes, it pays to do the dirty work. One of the hardest things to do is to convince an employee to take a job she doesn't want to do. I've had a lot of those moments. When I was at *The Wall Street Journal,* I moved to Boston to work for *The Boston Globe.* No one understood why I was doing it. Why leave the Yankees? Well, first of all, I had nonbusiness reasons for the move. Second, I was bored with what I was doing at the *Journal.* Usually, after four years, I get the itch. I also knew I wasn't one of the *Journal* stars. At the *Globe,* I could show my stuff. And it led to an editor's job—I was never an editor before—and that led to *Newsweek,* which led to *Fortune,* which all resulted in bigger and bigger paychecks and, of course, this book.

Even after I arrived at *Fortune,* I applied the theory of small roles. I was at *Fortune* for a year or so and didn't much like it. I was doing the same work I'd been doing at *Newsweek* and wasn't keen on doing the same job. My boss knew this and I'm pretty sure he didn't much care. But he had a little idea that maybe he should give me something else to do—at least while he was paying me. I inherited a small business magazine called *Your Company,* later *Fortune Small Business,* which, as I mentioned elsewhere in this book, was sent to small business credit card holders.

But I couldn't wait to be there. No one at Time Inc. cared much about it, as long as it made money or was on its way to making money. I could publish the stories I wanted when I wanted to publish them. I would get to fire the people I didn't like and hire people I did like. It was like a college newspaper.

We just had a lot of fun and produced a lot of good work. What's not to like? Do the work you enjoy, under the radar, and get paid major-league wages. Without any major-league headaches! This was my sales speech to potential employees. When they'd ask something like: "Why should I leave *Newsweek*? Nobody knows who you guys are." Well, at least for me, it got me places I didn't think I would ever go. For one thing, I ended up as a deputy at *Fortune*. If I didn't have a place to show those kinds of skills, I would never, ever have been offered that job. Never.

Patience in Small Roles

The Small Roles Theory works well even when you have a job. Few people get it, of course. They want to move up, especially younger workers, when they feel like they're ready. In their mind, anyway. When I became a deputy editor at *Fortune*, one of the first conversations I had was with an ultra-ambitious man who basically thought I—that's right, ME—was the wrong guy for the job. He believed I had just been handed the job he deserved and worked hard for. But he worked at it so hard that he alienated his bosses and took himself, as a result, out of the running. So we had a nice lunch. He explained his views of the magazine and what direction it should be going in. It was clear the next thing he was going to say—or wanted to, anyway—was "I was the right man for the deputy's job; I can't understand how you got it." I stopped him before it got to that.

"How old are you?" I asked.

"Thirty-five," he said.

"So why the hell are you in such a rush?" I asked. "Why don't you calm down and enjoy what you're doing instead of always vying for the next big job? You edit interesting stories, write interesting stories, and get paid a lot of money at a national publication. Why can't you just wait and accept your role? You'll get to run a magazine one day, or have my job, before you even hit forty."

He eventually left the magazine, but I think he left a little more patient than he was the day I had lunch with him. He's a very successful writer now. I don't think he would have ended up in the same place if he didn't accept what he thought was a smaller role.

With younger employees, it is especially tough to keep them patient and focused on what they're doing. At *Fortune*, we employed a woman we really wanted to keep at the magazine. She had tons of "upside," as they say. But she was frustrated, as young people at national magazines often are. They like the idea of the big brand name. They like wearing the badge. But they have absolutely no patience when it comes to paying dues for more than a couple of years.

This young writer was anxious to learn how to be a writer of long, narrative, deeply reported features. She didn't feel she was getting there at *Fortune*. I told her a big mistake people make is they move on too quickly, sometimes just before everything clicks. I asked her to be a little more patient. She agreed and was somewhat more successful in the following year. She eventually left, a couple of years after that conversation. But she was happy she worked hard at the smaller tasks and stayed. How do I know this? I asked her.

Director's Cut

☛ I've discussed a lot of big topics in this book—all of which I felt deserved several pages of explanation. But there are also a few other points I want to make before I let you go on your way. Consider this the "director's cut" section of the book—all of those lessons that may have interrupted, or just ruined, the flow of the rest of the book but are still worth sharing. Why? Because I think they are. And it's my book.

Are Gurus Worth It?

I have always been suspicious of "professional development" seminars. I get a lot of requests from employees about going to things like "accounting for journalists" or "business for business journalists." I usually let them go, largely because I'm weak and HR folks tell me I ought to support professional development, as they call it. They usually come back knowing little about accounting—or business for that matter. But they think they do, so I suppose it's all okay. (They also get the bug to go back to grad school. That's a good thing if you know they're not going to work out anyway.)

I pretty much feel that way about motivational speakers and their programs. We, meaning my company, once brought in former basketball star and businessman Magic Johnson to speak to a group of our salespeople. He talked about how playing basketball—focus, intensity, practice, blah and blah—produced lessons that can be applied to business. All I could think, when he was in the middle of his spiel, was how Magic, many years ago, got away with a foul to grab a crucial game-turning rebound against my team, the Boston Celtics. (What was that lesson, Magic?) I was really hoping that our sales folks weren't getting anything out of this because if they were, I was really going to start worrying, I have to tell you. None of us were/are six foot nine, let alone one of the greatest basketball players of all time. That was never going to change, so why the hell should I take this seriously?

The gold standard for this stuff is Tom Peters. He wrote a classic book—the great *In Search of Excellence*—and other books that were kind of classics but mostly variations on the original. He stole from himself, in other words, which I don't think is a bad thing. The Beatles did it. The Stones did it. This is no knock on Peters. I just find it strange that anyone would think he or she could become a great manager by attending one of his seminars. It's one of the great mysteries of business and human behavior. Tens of thousands of people go to these every year.

I remember attending, as a reporter, one of Tom's seminars when he was at the peak of his powers back in the eighties. He was talking about Sam Walton and how he built Wal-Mart and became known as a management genius. I looked around the room, which was mostly filled with middle-aged executives who looked like I look now and seemed desperate for any bit of information that could free them from the tyranny of middle management. (Maybe I was projecting. I was around thirty-five at the time and had given up on that hope a long time ago.) The audience was transfixed. Tom talked about how hard Sam worked and how he got the edge on his competitors and learned from each and every one of them.

Here's the thing. I knew Sam Walton, from the perspective of a journalist. There was nothing like him. His instincts were extraordinary, as was his drive. There was only one Sam Walton, like there is only one Michael Jordan, and you know what, folks? You aren't either one of them. At least most of you aren't. You can't duplicate what Walton did. I'm not even sure you could even learn one damn thing from him you could employ. (Well, I learned one thing. If you weren't selling as many batteries as you stocked, you should probably stock fewer batteries. Or at least display them better. When I open my battery store, this will help.)

Think about it. Sam Walton took a common concept, the store, and became a billionaire off of it. His money shot was bringing big-league retailing to the hinterlands and employing state-of-the-art distribution systems, which he was talked into by another Wal-Mart executive, David Glass. You aren't going to do that. You may do something else big, but not that, and most likely, whatever you do, it won't be written about for generations or discussed in management seminars.

But Walton does provide us a hell of a story and he did great things that make for good seminar fodder. You leave these events with a bunch of "best practices" and then you fall into your old habits within a day. A return to corporate schlubdom. But most executives have to feel like they can do something to make them better, so I guess it's okay to dream. It's like going to a U2 concert. You'll never play like them but at least you'll be entertained and get better at air guitar. I've come to the conclusion that people always feel like they're one good idea away from becoming great themselves. It's what got utility players in baseball in trouble. They thought they could become rich by taking steroids and becoming what they were not: home run hitters. (Whoops, they were right!)

In any event, the Tom Peters seminars were, and still are, I suppose, smart and entertaining. That's what you get out of them. And a couple of days off from work.

Can You Teach Employees to Be Entrepreneurs?

This is something that comes up a lot: that managers and employees should be more entrepreneurial. Instead of just doing their jobs, they're supposed to come up with new ideas for side businesses and, in my case, new kinds of editorial acts (like lists—my business just loves lists; you know, the top 50 Jewish CEOs, that kind of thing). We're expected to be entrepreneurial. It's like that in other big companies. Managers are in love with the idea of being "entrepreneurial." The trouble is most people will never be entrepreneurs. It's not in their DNA. Can you teach this?

It's just another one of those stupid debates that people in business have. There are schools all over the country that charge a lot of money and claim they can do it. But don't believe it for a minute. If you're young and want to be an entrepreneur—or be more entrepreneurial within the context of a big company—you can learn business skills for sure. But starting a business—and surviving the miserable failures along the way—takes a certain kind of character. First of all, you have to have a death wish. Most businesses are going to fail. Most ideas you pitch to your boss are going to fail. Can you work under that pressure?

My friend Paul McGoldrick is a painting contractor. I usually see him every week and ask how business is. It's either great or he doesn't know where his next dime will come from. How do you live like that? Paul usually says, "The business will come," and shrugs and goes off to practice his golf swing. I know his wife doesn't feel that way. But if you run your own business *you have to know the business will come.*

George Rosenbaum was one of the principals in the research firm Leo J. Shapiro & Associates in Chicago. I talked about running a small business with him years ago. His company has been around for decades. He says they have never had more than six months of business. If the expression "It is what it is" had been in vogue two decades ago, that's what George would say. That cold-blooded, I-don't-give-a-shit attitude can't be taught. It's part of you or not. The ability to live without the comfort of receivables is a skill. And if you improve your handicap, all the better.

I'm not sure why people think they can do it easily or be taught how to do it. Come up with a good idea, and you're set—right? Well, it's like this. When I was a third grader, I wondered why margarine was so hard and why it couldn't be soft so I could spread it on bread. Great idea—eh? Only I was in the third grade and I had no idea how to become a soft margarine mogul. Well, most adults are like that. They have great ideas and don't know how to execute them. They'll always be third graders when it comes to starting businesses.

You have to have the idea, know how to execute the idea, be willing to mortgage your home to pay for your new business, and not stress out one tiny bit about the prospects of failure. (The corporate version? Come up with a bad idea; cost your company a lot of money; get fired.) You think Fred Smith was worried about failure when he started Federal Express? Sure, a little, I suppose. But I don't think he had any doubt he could do it. I met a guy named Bruce Williams a few years back for a story I was working on about talk radio "money advisers." He was a radio host who ran a talk show "about life" (one of the nation's biggest talk shows at the time). A lot of the time he fielded calls from listeners who had various schemes for starting businesses. For example: "I have an idea to sell dog food from a mall kiosk. Think that's a good idea, Bruce?" Well, Bruce was a kind guy, and would go over all these things you have to do to start a pet food business. Insurance, inventory, market research, you name it. "They usually never do a thing. They just liked to talk about it," Bruce told me. It was small business porn for them.

When Sorry's Not Enough—or Inappropriate, Anyway

If you're a boss, pay attention to this. They don't want you to say you're sorry. They don't. They don't. Get it? Don't fire someone and say, "This was so hard for me because you're such a great guy." Don't tell them how hard the latest round of layoffs was for you. Don't look depressed. You're the guy keeping his job. Just say good-bye and make sure they get all the severance they have coming to them. If they can have their health insurance stretched out, do that. Tell them you'll write a recommendation for them. Just don't play the victim. THEY HATE YOU! Listening is helpful but can get a little stressful if you think someone is going to go off on you. My boss knows people he fires hate him. He was talking with a reporter he just let go and let him have his say . . . and let him have his say . . . and let him have his say. He just kept repeating the same thing over and over again. How he was doing a good job; how he was on the verge of some big story; how we didn't manage him properly. Then he started scratching the bottom of his ankle as he talked and became a little agitated. My boss thought he was going for a gun or a knife, which would have been interesting. It turned out to be just an itch. But still, the guy was in no mood for his boss to whine about having to fire him.

Can You Measure the Output of Creative Folks?

You know what? I hate consulting firms. I really do. One such firm recommended sending copyediting tasks to India. I kid you not. It is not only part of the consulting world's playbook—outsourcing is its favorite thing ever—but these recommendations are made by many people who, my guess is, have never worked on the street.

Number crunchers in the publishing world have taken, and probably still take, the number of words writers produce and divide it by their pay and benefits. This calculation determines how much you're costing the company per word. This theory is so full of holes I don't know where to start. But let's start this way: it's like saying one page of prose written by one of my top writers is the same as a page produced by a kid just out of high school. I realize this could happen, but it's unlikely.

During one round of layoffs a number of years ago I tried to explain to one of my business managers how writers work. In a creative process like writing, you have twenty people working on stories based on good ideas. Maybe five of those stories will come out great. Let's say you cut the staff by 30 percent. What happens? Fewer great stories. And the last time I checked, you're still charging advertisers and subscribers the same rate. So who is the loser here? Pick any business. It's the same. Advertising, computers, Big Pharma. It's hard to measure creative productivity by the numbers. But careers and consulting group fees are based on that, so there you have it.

It still amazes me that business folks in a creative business don't understand this. I kind of blame the bonus culture for this. If your compensation is based on how the company's finances will do in any one year, are you going to listen to someone like me? No chance in hell. It's what's going on with the Internet and journalism right now, with some important exceptions, of course. The pay is hideous, so in comparison with what's done at magazines like *Fortune* and *The New Yorker* and *The New York Times Magazine*, it's Shangri-la for consulting types.

✖

The Cult of Jack Welch

I always liked the idea of Jack Welch. A fire-breathing, take-no-prisoners chief executive who demanded the best of his employees. One of his more controversial theories was that cutting the bottom portion of your workforce every year will increase productivity. Get rid of the "C" players in other words. This is now embraced by way too many managers. Is it wrong to think that way? Not entirely. I think it's good to try to constantly bring in good people and let people go who you just know have no future. Welch is long gone from GE, but his scheme still comes up a lot. Well, you have to wonder in this day and age whether it works at all. As one reader at Welch's Web site pointed out, the program doesn't work at all if you don't replace the "C"s you fired. Because if you cut back year after year, you'll eventually slash your "A" and "B" players if you don't replace the workers you're firing, which happens at a lot of companies. You'll also have a workforce so obsessed with making the cut that they'll turn on each other.

And it may have the opposite effect. People won't try harder to be better. They'll avoid taking chances for fear of failing. Here's a take from one of Welch's Web site readers: "There is another danger," the reader wrote. "That the fear of being in the bottom . . . will encourage [people to avoid] standing out from the crowd. Company recruitment advertisements . . . demand 'out of the box thinking.' But who is more likely to come up with more innovative ideas? Is it the raucous group that discusses the same television programs every morning, drinks together every night and heads off en masse to play in the chairman's golf challenge each spring? Or are the new ideas more likely to come from Joe in the corner, who doesn't say much and is more likely to be labeled a 'C.'"

Can't say I agree with all of that. But the Welch rule just ain't that simple. Two of the people who had their say earlier in this book weighed in on this subject. Chicago consultant Sam Hill says such a system sometimes forces people to focus on not only their careers, but the careers of others. All in the name of survival. "Any place where survival is highly rewarded encourages people not to speak up," says Hill. What can happen? "It always encourages you to trip the guy when he's not looking."

Sam has a good point. I've seen certain editors, trying to undermine anyone who might be seen as competition, deliberately let things they know aren't exactly right appear in stories. Then they'd point this out to the boss. They'd look good; their rival would look bad.

Not quite sure that's a good thing for the customers.

I'm pretty sure that's not what Jack Welch was out to achieve at GE. Bill Conaty, the former GE human resources chief, thinks that the GE/Welch system is misunderstood. "Differentiation of talent breeds meritocracy and treating everyone the same breeds mediocrity. I believe that rewarding and recognizing your best performers while simultaneously taking corrective action on your less effective employees is a smart and honest way to improve your business performance." The key, he adds, is to let every employee know where they stand and what they need to do to get to the next level.

Or survive, I guess. Can't say I can argue with that.

Large Meetings in Small Doses Only

I hate meetings. I hate the idea of meetings. I hate being in meetings. I hate the performance art of meetings. I hate people who perfect the art of meetings. I hate people who do well in meetings, even though I know they have good intentions. I hate what meetings do to people who are shy and the impact that they have on people's careers. I really hate how much time they waste. A little Q&A with myself.

Q: *When did you start hating meetings?*
A: It goes back to high school. I always dreaded the time in class when teachers would call on me to explain the third chapter of Conrad's *Heart of Darkness*. Just give me a test and grade it, okay? We don't have to talk about it in class. I really didn't like watching other kids stand up and talk about *Heart of Darkness* either. Painful. Almost as bad as PowerPoints. Well, I shouldn't go that far. Some of the kids were really good at presenting so I hated the process (and them) even more.

Q: *When you became a manager, when did you notice you really didn't like such gatherings?*
A: At *The Boston Globe*. We had morning meetings. We had afternoon meetings. The newspaper's editor just asked about the stories that we were working on. He went from editor to editor until we ran out of ideas for doodles. Could have all been done by e-mail. I was never great at it. I didn't command the room. I didn't sound like I knew what I was talking about. But I really did. Trust me, I needed a deeper voice.

Q: *Do you think it ever hurt your career?*
A: Sure. When I was in talks with *Newsweek,* this was the single most discussed topic. "We're a meeting culture, we're a little worried you won't thrive in it." Why would they assume that? They wouldn't say much except I was soft-spoken. The problem was I looked young for my age, had a highish voice. I wasn't from *Newsweek* central casting, which ground out tall journalists with deep voices and their radios tuned to NPR's *All Things Considered.* (I listened to Howard Stern and Don Imus, depending on my mood. The rest of them eventually caught up to me on that.)

Q: *What's the secret of good meetings?*
A: Less is more may be a cliché, but it's true. We have a meeting every morning. Other than my boss having some of the best comedy material in the business, we don't get a whole lot accomplished. Meetings have to have a specific purpose. Meetings have to have the right people in the room. I go meeting-crazy when I look around the room and see people who have absolutely nothing to contribute. They sit mute. A peanut gallery. I think they're there to provide a laugh track. You also have to have meetings that are fairly quick. Get the work done. Get out. Also have fewer of them. There has been a tradition at *Fortune* that the editor has to tell funny stories. When I'm boss, I'm going to hire Carrot Top.

Q: *Come on, some meetings must be useful. . . .*
A: The after-meeting meetings are useful. That's when things break up and you just talk about anything that comes to mind. Then you stumble, invariably, into an important topic and you get work done. Always happens. So if you want to have a good

meeting, end the old one quickly and just hang out. Quick, single-topic meetings with a small group are good, too.

Q: *What was your favorite meeting ever?*
A: Well, I don't know if it was my favorite, but it was the sickest. When I was at *Newsweek,* we flew off to Steamboat Springs, Colorado, to have an "offsite" for the managers and some of the top writers. One evening, we were sitting around the fireplace and the boss, who was drunk, shouted out, "Who should we fire?" So he went around the room and asked each of us who on the staff should be fired and why. The other editors named a few of my people. So I spent most of my time defending the business writers and avoided choosing others. I basically refused to participate. A pretty obnoxious scene. Probably conjured up by a management consultant. I did ride on a dogsled for the first time at the offsite, so it wasn't totally a waste.

Why I Hate Focus Groups

At some point at the publication I work at, we decide to "reevaluate our mission." So we conduct focus groups. Now, I'm not a big fan of focus groups. And I'm probably not right about despising them, but hear me out anyway. For one thing, you're dealing with a group of people who willingly abandon their families for a couple of hundred dollars and free food. Remember, most upscale readers and what we call "prospects" aren't going hungry. So right off the bat you have to be suspicious.

Another problem: they all want to sound smarter than maybe they really are. ("Of course I read that article on behavioral economics. It was terrific.") Finally, I've seen a number of focus groups over the past couple of decades. They always say the same thing. They want more stories "I can apply to my own business life. I want more stories that speak to me." Well, first of all, you really can't do that. Go buy a trade magazine like Rubber Manufacturers Illustrated if you want to get down to that kind of detail. (By the way, that magazine doesn't exist. But it should.)

We come out of those sessions with what you might expect. The readers like deeply reported stories and also enjoy the smaller, service-oriented pieces. They always say that. We could have come up with that answer and saved a lot of money. But, as I said, what do I know? You'd go broke if you left me in charge of any publishing operation.

It's Not You, It's Who You Work for, Stupid

I don't know about your business, but in my profession a lot of people think they're important because, well, they're so great. Of course, it has *nothing* to do with the organization they work for. They could just leave *The New York Times* and have the same juice. Sometimes that's true. For the stars. For most of us, let me clue you in on something: the next person in your job will be just as important as you are. My favorite story about this is from an old dear friend, who passed away a few years back. His name was Stanley Slom and he was an editor of a magazine at a trade publisher, Lebhar-Friedman, where I worked in the early eighties. Stan was previously at *The Wall Street Journal,* where he covered retailing. And everybody in the business knew him and, in a way, feared him. Because he worked for *The Wall Street Journal.* He took a job at Lebhar-Friedman's *Chain Store Age* and all that changed. He tried calling Toys "R" Us founder and CEO Charles Lazarus for a story. Charles wouldn't return his calls. (You have to understand: writers at trade magazines always have problems getting phone calls returned. That's not a bad thing. It makes you a tougher aid and a harder-working reporter.) Stan finally ran into Lazarus at a trade show and confronted him.

"Charles," Stan told me he said, "why haven't you returned my calls? I thought we were friends."

"Sorry, Stan," Lazarus said. "You don't work for *The Wall Street Journal* anymore. You can't do anything for me now." Stan Slom was back to being Stan Slom again. A nice, smart man; a very good journalist. But he didn't carry *The Wall Street Journal* business card anymore. So much for returned phone calls.

I was thirty years old at the time. More than two decades later, Stan's story still haunts me. I know when I leave *Fortune* my kids will go out and find a new dad at another national media organization.

Gen Y, Whatever

Baby boomer managers, like me, are for some reason obsessed with a class of workers who belong to the group known as "Generation Y." It's as if they, the children of baby boomers, are another form of life. They are, the story line goes, generally self-centered; don't give up their independence easily; want to know what their employers can do for them; like money but don't like money that much; are looking for "meaningful" relationships; and think work life is one big extension of the college campus experience.

Kind of like their parents, though a lot smarter, truth be told. This generation of workers has watched a lot of people get laid off—like their parents—and don't trust employers at all. They know there are not a lot of job opportunities, at least in my business. The Gen Y-ers are, for sure, not as loyal, and I can't say they're wrong to be that way. It's not enough that you have a job at a big, prestigious company. That doesn't cut it. If I had to generalize about my experience with this group, they need to see where they are going in the company—and their careers. All the time. I want to be like them.

When I grew up in the newspaper business, I lived in fear of losing my job. I lived in fear of leaving *The Wall Street Journal.* My identity was all wrapped up in it. What would I say at parties if I left? How was I going to impress people if I wasn't working for a branded media organization? I wasn't all that impressive in real life. It was all I had! Look around at any old-school publication. There are still people holding on because they worry about this stuff. A lot. This is a sad story. I read a few years ago about a New York media veteran who struggled with depression. He was fiftysomething and at that point of his career was working the night shift. I could relate to that. I imagined that he was desperately hanging on, being unhappy, partly because he wanted that big media badge.

The Gen Y kids aren't like that. If they're unhappy, they'll find something else to do. Since I've been at *Fortune,* we've had talented kids go to work for museums, PR agencies, the CIA (I suspect anyway), and even start their own businesses. No damn way they were going to wait a decade to see what happens. The Gen Y-ers don't want to wake up in their mid- to late thirties in a job that's not going anywhere. That's what their parents did.

As a boss, it took me a while to catch on to this. I don't have a whole lot of patience for the touchy-feely part of my job, but the Gen Y-ers on the staff kind of forced it on me. I had one young writer who, every couple of months, would come into my office and almost plead with me to tell her the secret to getting a story into *Fortune.* "Well," I said, "read the magazine. Those, obviously, are the types of stories that make it in." I thought, at first, she wasn't all that smart about our business. But I finally figured out she was testing me in a way—trying to figure out if this was the kind of place where she was comfortable. Is this an editor who will mentor me? (Uh, no.) In other words, "Do I want to stay at *Fortune*?" Well, she didn't, and thank goodness, because she wasn't all that good.

But that's not the point. She was doing what every other person her age was doing: testing her boss. I was finally getting it.

So what's the best way to deal with Gen Y-ers? How do you get them to stay? I talked with Nadira Hira, who is writing a book on the subject. Nadira used to work for me at *Fortune* and is, as far as I am concerned, the go-to person when it comes to the new generation of workers and what makes them tick. She's also the prototype Gen Y-er in the workplace: really smart, with lots of opinions about everything. If management (me) was doing something that made Nadira and other young folks unhappy, she'd tell me about it. Now—just between us—she took the complaints of colleagues who were much less talented than she was a little too seriously. If they were unhappy, Nadira was unhappy. And sometimes they were right. (A good part of their unhappiness was that they weren't suited to big-time journalism and hadn't quite come to terms with that yet. But I'll take the blame for the rest.)

I wanted to know more, so I asked Nadira if she would talk a little about the generation she belonged to. These are edited excerpts, meaning that the questions and answers are massaged a bit and do not necessarily appear in their original order.

> HG: I have a theory that Gen Y-ers are smarter than their baby boom parents. They won't linger in a job that isn't for them. They want to be happy more than anything else. Also, they don't, wisely, trust anyone. Is that a good theory or am I suffering from the "I'm really smart and insightful in my own mind" syndrome?

> NH: Believe it or not, a few people have this theory, too. It may not be so much that we're smarter than our baby boom parents but rather that we've learned from them. How many of us have had parents who've been laid off from a company where they've spent decades, or won't be able to retire for years because of all that's happened on

Wall Street? So we're not going to be loyal to institutions that aren't loyal to us. And we certainly won't put off living life for a retirement that may never come. Our parents were the "live to work" generation. Which doesn't mean, by the way, that we don't care about work or we do it for the paycheck. Quite the opposite, in fact. For us, work has to be an integrated part of life. It has to reflect our values and our goals. And, ultimately, it has to reward us in meaningful ways—not just in terms of wallet or ego. That means we're going to give a lot, but we're going to expect to get a lot, too. And as far as I'm concerned, it's about time.

HG: What kind of advice would you give employers on dealing with Gen Y-ers? Please help me.

NH: Talk to them. I think the most powerful tool any employer has with Gen Y-ers is conversation. When it comes to work, we're looking for great relationships, great opportunities, and a great mission. And any worthwhile company can offer that. But we don't know that about your company—and you don't help us see that by facilitating some real-life social networking, structuring some proper career planning, and engaging us all to be partners in meeting that mission—it isn't worth anything at all.

What's more, if there's an atmosphere of conversation, it can help the whole company face challenges more effectively. Employees are less likely to skip out during hard times. And a lot more will give you the benefit of the doubt if they know and trust you. So managers need to be in constant dialogue with their Y-ers.

HG: You mentioned in a *Fortune* cover story on Gen Y-ers that one job prospect brought a parent along during the tour of his new workplace. It was in our magazine, so I know it happened. But I want to believe it really didn't happen. You have to blame the baby boomer parent for that one, right?

NH: Of course it happened! I just did a lecture at a big aerospace company and one of the folks told me about a mom who called him to accept a job offer he extended to her child. As crazy as it sounds, don't think that's so unusual. That doesn't make it right. Resist the urge to parent your children right into retirement, and let them learn how to live on their own. But realize, as a manager, that parents can sometimes be an ally in getting or keeping good young talent. And that's why the company in my story invited the parent to the orientation in the first place. So if your Y-er shows up with Mom or Dad to the holiday party, don't be surprised.

[AUTHOR'S NOTE: I find this, I'm sorry, to be crazy. My parents did show up at my Little League games but had no idea when I was taking my SAT. Nor were they even involved in the college process. "You're going to Arizona State? That's nice, dear."]

HG: So, when old guys like me interview young people like you, what should we expect?

NH: Some Y-ers will come in with résumés full of internships that amount to more job experience than you have, while others have expectations that are so out of whack with reality that you'll be left speechless. So don't let anything shock you and try to look beyond anything that does. This is a generation that has been taught to speak up. So we may say things in interviews about what we want for ourselves or what we've heard about your company that many veteran employees wouldn't bring up. It may give you an advantage in hiring someone who can think critically and give you an honest opinion.

It may also happen that if you present a Y-er with a tough situation in an interview, you'll find some of them will lose all that cachet they had on paper and become flustered. That's not unusual with this generation, which is used to handling conflict via text message. So recognize that communication gaps are a generational challenge that your managers will have to help them face. And don't get me started about the person who wears jeans to an interview. That's not ideal, but it doesn't mean there isn't an awesome employee somewhere in that denim. So try to keep an open mind and, by all means, think of how your kids would fare in the same situation.

Sometimes You Just Have to Tell Them to Stick a Sock in It

I was dying to put this story somewhere in the book. But I couldn't find a place for it because it just isn't my style. But I had to. Shortly after I accepted a job at *Fortune,* I was asked to attend an all-hands staff meeting at the Women's National Republican Club. I don't recall why the meeting was scheduled and I have no idea what the Women's National Republican Club is and what they, the members, do there. The event took place around fourteen years ago. Times were good. The staff was big. I was the new guy sitting in the audience.

I figured everyone was basically happy. I mean, what the hell was there to be unhappy about? (At work, at least.) You know, they all had great jobs, business was booming, and they got to work for one of the great titles in journalism. But there's always a small crowd that loves to complain. Just coming from *Newsweek,* I understood that all too well. So, soon into the meeting, one writer got up and started to whine about morale. I can't even remember what the problem was. The cafeteria? There was no champagne in the limos on the way home from work? He had to work more than three days a week? Who knows? The speaker's complainathon went on for about ten minutes or so. There was a pause. *Fortune*'s then managing editor, John Huey, looked around the room without saying a word. Then he talked. "You know," he said, "I think good morale is overrated." That was it. The complainer sat down and we were on to the next question. It was a brilliant comeback. For most of the editorial folks in the room, John's response was a relief. They liked their jobs and didn't much cotton to whiners. But John's message, my theory anyway, was this: "For all you unhappy people in the audience, it may be time to move on." And he was right.

Postscript

It's been a couple of years since I first thought about what would eventually become the introduction to this book, and even more time has passed since I conjured up the basic story lines while driving back from a movie with my son Kyle. I really have no idea, to this day, why these ideas came to me during that short ride home. It was a flow-of-consciousness thing, I think. I had just seen *Paul Blart: Mall Cop* and, being me, started thinking that's what I was going to end up doing if I didn't survive the media's latest layoffathon. (So thanks, Kevin James, for that inspirational performance.)

But a lot has changed since then, so I thought I'd leave you with some of my insights since I started on this modest journey.

First off, the media revolution, which has been a big challenge managementwise for a lot of us, continues. And, to you tell you the truth, most of the changes are actually good. Forget about the layoffs for a second. It's becoming increasingly clear that words, reporting, and storytelling are what really matter to readers, because that's how you make yourself different and provide value. The distribution system doesn't matter. The iPad, iPhone, iMac, who cares? Good journalism is just good. There are problems, of course. There's the moving-too-fast-to-care-about-accuracy thing. There's the hype-for-Web-traffic thing. But, hell. I truly believe that the excitement of all this change is really attracting good people to the profession and giving some folks, who might have been shut out of our business when there were only print products around, a chance to show their stuff to a national audience. I can't prove that, but I stand by it.

And no matter how we produce and deliver things, the basics of good management remain. If you got this far in the book—or just read books Hebrew-style—let me leave you with a couple of thoughts. For one thing, no matter what your management style, it will work if you do it well, are honest, treat your employees with respect, and are consistent. I can't believe I'm actually saying stuff like this, but trust me, it does work in real life. Now, I don't pretend my personal style is for everyone—I'm not a hard-ass, football-coach type; I'm not particularly clever and I'm not smart enough to have hidden agendas and pit folks against each other. (As fun as that may sound.) I have, though some might disagree, a "nice guy management style." Like anyone else, I get angry and act like an idiot. But mostly I get my way by being, well, friendly. I still believe that's the way to go. The most talented folks won't stay with you long if you act like a drill sergeant. They don't have to.

I also want to point out that I don't claim to do everything right. I break my own rules from time to time, like everyone else. So if you're one of my current or former employees who want to pick this book apart because I once did something to you that doesn't follow my own advice, don't bother. I know! I'm a multiple offender. But I like to think I've learned a lot along the way.

✖

Do I still like management after more than two decades? I'll tell you what I don't like. I don't like having to fire people who are having problems in their lives; I don't like listening to people complain about something that the expense account cops got on their case about; I don't like having to tell folks to find another career because they're not talented. (That's what I miss about being a writer—worrying only about yourself.) But there's nothing better than working out a story idea with a great journalist or helping someone get over a particularly hard time in her career. Recently, a great writer on the *Fortune* staff who was in the middle of a bad case of writer's angst told me how he sometimes felt like he was a worthless slug of a journalist who was totally devoid of talent. (That about sums up what it's like to be a writer, actually.) I got to ease his pain a bit. "No, you're not worthless. You're actually pretty good and your stories always turn out great." (I believed that; I hope he did.) I didn't know how to do that kind of thing when I started; I know how to do that now. And even after twenty years, it keeps me coming back to work.

But to really answer the question, I'll leave you with the words of one of the wisest people I've ever met. In the late eighties and early nineties, my wife and I used to shop at an antiques store called Aunt Wren's, located in Supply, a small town on the southeast coast of North Carolina. There was really an Aunt Wren. (At least the owner of the shop said she was Aunt Wren.) She was, I guess, in her midseventies at the time and had a great North Carolina drawl. One weekend we visited the shop and, as I usually did, I asked Aunt Wren how business was going, how she was feeling, and how the world was treating her. "Well, honey," she said, "more good than bad." That kind of sums up management— for me.

✖

Acknowledgments

☛ This is the hardest part of the book for me, believe it or not, because I'm terrified of forgetting to thank someone who has helped me out along the way. So let's just get it over with.

First to thank—this is an easy one—is my family: my partner in crime and wife, Catherine, and sons Kevin, Eddie, and Kyle. I'd like to say they made all these sacrifices while I worked on this book on weekends and vacations. But the truth is, they always seem to have a good time whether I'm involved or not. They are pretty cool, that's really all I can say. Other than mentioning that I'd be lost without them.

There are a slew of people who helped me with content and advice. Super-consultant and fellow writer Sam Hill not only appears in this book, with some great stuff on dealing with evil, micromanaging bosses, but actually found an agent for me. (That would be Lorin Rees; more on him later.) Howard Schultz of Starbucks was gracious enough to give me material he could have saved exclusively for his own book, which may be available as you read this. (Please buy it!) Jim Collins, one of the gods of management thought and research, came out of his self-described writing "cave" to give me, and the readers of this book, a lot to think about. Norm Pearlstine, a former boss at *The Wall Street Journal* and Time Inc.—and now a rival at *Bloomberg BusinessWeek*—refreshed my memory about some important events over the years.

I've always been interested in sports and the dynamics of putting together a successful team. So thanks to Kansas City Chiefs general manager Scott Pioli, one of the best minds in professional football or any profession. I didn't use a whole lot from my interviews with him, but our discussions certainly influenced my thinking. Bill Conaty, General Electric's legendary HR man, and Ram Charan, the world's ultimate CEO coach, also provided some good advice and material. (And did I mention they are coauthors of a book called *The Talent Masters*?)

A *Fortune* writer, the very talented Mina Kimes, also did a wonderful job compiling business lists for me ("Best TV Bosses," and similar things) that didn't make the final cut. But if I ever do a director's cut of this book's "Director's Cut" chapter, you'll find the lists very amusing. Also a bow to *Fortune* master librarian Marilyn Adamo, who helped me with an important clip search or two.

You absolutely cannot produce an acknowledgments section without mentioning folks who helped you professionally. Special thanks to Steve Bailey, now of Bloomberg, who took a chance and gave me my first editor's job at *The Boston Globe*. Some people at the *Globe* thought he was crazy and they were probably right. I'm glad he wasn't fired. My bosses at *Fortune*/Time Inc., John Huey and Andy Serwer, were very supportive of this little project. (I suspect they were basically humoring me, but I've been afraid to ask.) They're the nazz, as we used to say in the seventies. Kathy Christensen, now a professor at the University of Nebraska, hired me at *The Wall Street Journal*. Really, thanks for that, Kathy. I learned more at the *Journal* in two weeks than I had in my whole career up to that point. And two of my journalism professors at the University of South Carolina deserve a very special thank-you: Henry Price and Pat McNeely. A lot of people can teach the technical aspects of the business; they got me jazzed about being a reporter.

Lorin Rees, of the Rees Literary Agency, in the world's greatest city, Boston, was my agent, but he was much more than that. (Not that there's anything wrong with being just an agent.) He was a smart editor and forced me to think things out before even trying to peddle this book. The team at Portfolio, the publisher, was terrific and the staff made this whole process so easy. Thanks, guys, especially the boss, Adrian Zackheim, for giving me such a great editor, Brooke Carey, who is going to be a star, and a fantastic publicist, Maureen Cole, who helped get the book noticed.

Finally, a few words for some friends and colleagues who listened to me whine about this whole thing so my family didn't have to. In no particular order: Walt Bogdanich, David Kaplan, Mia Diehl, Nancy Cooper, Brian Dumaine, Alix Colow, James Bandler, Tim Smith, Nadira Hira, Jennifer Reingold, and Peter Elkind. And thank-you, Richard and Leslie Weinfeld and Jill and Michael Kajouras, who welcomed me to Louisville, and Cliff Cohen from the great northern Washington suburbs. I wrote a big chunk of this book in both places. A special thanks to Lynn's Paradise Café in Louisville, Barnes and Noble in Cortlandt Manor, New York, and the Peekskill Coffee House in Peekskill, New York, for letting me spend hours in their establishments. They didn't make much money on me.

Whew, that's it. If I missed anyone, forgive me.

—HANK GILMAN, SEPTEMBER 30, 2010

Index